Other Books by
VICTORIA BOOTH DEMAREST

A Violin, A Lily, and You
1976

Alive and Running
Devotions for Active People
1976

King David
1964

What I Saw In Europe
1953

Shade of His Hand
A Book of Consolation
1941, 1963

The Holy Spirit
1927

Broken Lives
1924

The Lily
1917

GOD, WOMAN & MINISTRY

Revised Edition
International Standard Book No. 0-912760-61-3
Library of Congress Catalog Card No. 76-42915

First Published in 1977

Published by

SACRED ARTS INTERNATIONAL, INC.

in cooperation with

2135 1ST AVENUE SOUTH
ST. PETERSBURG, FLORIDA 33712

GOD, WOMAN & MINISTRY

by VICTORIA BOOTH DEMAREST

PHOTOGRAPHS BY
SACRED ARTS INTERNATIONAL, INC.

Victoria Booth-Clibborn in the early days of her career.

A Sacred Arts International Photograph

Where there is no vision the people perish
—Proverbs 29:18

Many congregations have never seen or heard a woman in the pulpit. Their image of woman as preacher and minister has never taken shape. They do not know what a valuable experience they are missing.

Sacred Arts International, Inc., is pleased to present, in this volume, words of wisdom written, in her eighties, by one of the most outstanding women ever to address a congregation.

May this volume reveal to its readers what woman, as preacher and minister, can contribute not only to their individual lives but to the service of humanity as well.

We have persuaded Reverend Demarest to permit us to include photographs to provide a visual image as well.

TABLE OF CONTENTS

S.A.I. Illustrations
on pages vi, xvii, 41, 61, 91, 108, 118, 126,
132, 140, 144, and 164.

INTRODUCTION

"Another book on the ministry of women?" you ask. No. This is not "another" book on anything. It is a deeply moving experience — of a different character entirely from the many fine and scholarly books about women which are being published in increasing numbers.

Though delightfully easy to read, this is also a scholarly book. Victoria Booth Demarest is a profound student of the Bible, as well as of the Church Fathers and of the best of modern theology. There are the marks of sound scholarship, adequate footnotes and solid documentation. But these are not what makes the book important and compelling.

Where else in the world is there a book written by a woman who has been an evangelist and a minister for over seventy years, and whose mother and grandmother were ministers and evangelists before her? As you read the book you will be caught up in the drama of this amazing family. The depths of their faith in God, their tragedies and triumphs, are the ingredients of which great drama is fashioned. It is as exciting as fiction — and it is all true! Don't read it if you are reluctant to have your heart and your mind touched and perhaps changed.

For church men and women, including those in positions of authority, it will raise many questions and provide convincing answers. For the many women of various denominations struggling with the question of their own vocations it will give the light of the experience of a woman who heeded a "call." It may reveal to some women the fact that theirs is not a commitment of sufficient depth. To others it may present a possibility and a glory which they had only dimly perceived.

Now in her eighty-sixth year, Mrs. Demarest has been witnessing, preaching, and counselling since she was a child. She has written many hymns, religious dramas, and other books. She had a world-wide reputation as an evangelist long before her ordination in the United Church of Christ in 1949. The granddaughter of William and Catherine Booth, founders of the Salvation Army; niece of the famous Evangeline Booth who long headed the Army in the United States; daughter of the woman who organized the Salvation Army in most of Western Europe, hers was a rich background. But the decision to embark on her own life of service and mission was in response to a deeply personal experience of God's call.

In reading the persuasive and heart-warming account of her own convictions and actions, one realizes that in writing this book she is, once again, responding to God's call. There is no other woman in the world today who could provide us with the information, inspiration, and guidance which Victoria Booth Demarest can give. That God has granted her the strength and ability to write it, at this time when it is so greatly needed, is surely a sign of His Grace.

—Cynthia C. Wedel, Ph.D.
Past President, National Council of Churches, USA. . .
Currently one of six presidents of the World Council
of Churches, elected at the
General Assembly, Nairobi, Kenya,

PREFACE

We are living in a time of world crisis. Winds of change are blowing through every sphere of human life, not the least of which is the spiritual. The universal church, catholic, orthodox and protestant, is also being shaken by these winds — one of which is the rising of women to demand that the rights granted to them on the day of Pentecost be recognized and restored.

Most of the major protestant denominations have agreed to ordain women. And, as this book goes to press, news comes that the great Episcopal church, which brings together both catholic and protestant elements, has voted to admit women to the orders of priests and bishops.

However, opposition to this development still exists throughout the universal church. All of those involved agree that the issue will be debated for years. As one Episcopal bishop commented, the decision of his church to ordain women may cause "irreversible despair and desperation to the hearts of many." In the words of another minister, "Something we know well and love is passing, and something is being born that we do not understand."

It is obvious that devout and sincere souls are suffering, still believing that the ordination of women is contrary to the will of God. It is with deep desire to comfort and reassure those who are troubled, while at the same time offering encouragement to women who feel called by God to become ministers or priests, that I have written this book.

When this controversy exploded into the much publicized ordination of eleven women as Episcopal priests on July 19, 1974, in Philadelphia, the ordaining Episcopal Bishops wrote: "This action is intended as an act of obedience to the [Holy] Spirit . . . hearing His command we can heed no other. We gladly join ourselves with *those* who in other times and places as well as here and now have sought obedience to that same Spirit."[1]

Since I am one of "those" I am happy to join my witness to theirs.

"Only *experience* can show the extent to which women might fulfill a useful role in the ordained ministry." So read a report prepared by the Committee to Study the Proper Place of Women in the Ministry of the Church. This Committee which had been appointed by the House of Bishops of the Episcopal Church,[2] decided in favor of the ordination of women priests.

Only experience!

To me the question of woman's ministry has spanned three generations of experience.

My grandmother, Catherine Mumford Booth,[3] a co-founder of the Salvation Army with her husband, William Booth, was, according to Maude Royden, "the most wonderful example of female Ministry on record."[4] Her four daughters followed in her footsteps as did her three sons. (See Appendix A)

While still in her twenties, the eldest of those daughters, my mother Catherine Booth-Clibborn ("The Maréchale"), carried the Salvation Army to France, Holland, and Switzerland — where she became the heroine of a famous trial and won a great victory for woman's right to preach.

I myself, born in Paris, France, have preached the Gospel for more than seventy years, in fourteen countries and in four languages, to congregations of all leading denominations, including Episcopal and Greek Orthodox. Never once have I questioned my right as a woman to preach or to minister. (In 1949 I was ordained a minister of the Congregational Church, now The United Church of Christ.)

It is my hope that the experience and insights gathered during these three generations, some of which are recorded in this book, will be of value to others, both men and women, who wish to devote their lives to the service of the Lord. More especially I hope that the book will provide encouragement to the many young women already preparing, in faith, for hoped-for careers as ministers or priests.

Theological scholars are familiar with the significant Biblical references to women and do not need to be reminded of them. But frequently I am questioned by concerned women whose sketchy Scriptural knowledge makes it difficult for them to discover, for themselves, the true facts pertaining to woman's equal right to preach the Gospel. For them I have sought to point out, as clearly as I could, what the Bible really tells us about the relationship of women to the church, and specifically, to the ministry.

It is high time for mistranslations and misapplications of the Scriptures, particularly of New Testament passages which disparage and denigrate woman, to be corrected. The public is entitled to know what the Bible really says about women. If truth and justice are to prevail, it would seem advisable for translators and commentators of the future to take into account the scholarly writings of certain men and women, preachers and ministers, on the question of woman's ministry. Especially should they take cognizance of the expert research of such scholars as Dr. Katherine Bushnell (*God's Word to Women*),[5] the Rev. Maude Royden (*The Church and Woman*)[4] and, particularly, Dr. Lee Anna Starr (*The Bible Status of Women*)[6]. The information these books contain makes it virtually impossible for sex prejudice or opposition to woman's ministry to remain in the mind of any honest person.

I am not speaking as a feminist, because the first priority of a Christian is not to seek the rights of woman or of man but rather to seek the rights of God and humanity. Men and women should mutually respect and admire each other. They only tarnish their own images when they assert their own superiority. For the creation of mankind both are needed equally. To be born into the world a baby needs a father and a mother, and, for healthy and normal development, the child continues to need both.

This principle applies also to the church, a body composed of men and women alike. Their needs cannot be fully met without the spiritual services and guidance of ministers of both sexes. This is discussed in Chapter Six.

At this point I would like to give recognition and honor to those men who, rather than oppose my ministry, gave to it the benefit of their respectful and enthusiastic support and cooperation. First, my husband, C. Agnew Demarest, who, to the end of his life, stood by me in all my efforts for the Kingdom. Then to the male ministers, too numerous to name, many of them outstanding in the Congregational, Baptist, Methodist, and Presbyterian denominations, who opened their churches to my city-wide evangelistic campaigns and individual preaching missions. To Dr. E. Stanley Jones, Methodist missionary, author and evangelist, and Dr. Frank Laubach, founder of "World Literacy," both of whom gave me much encouragement. To the Archbishop of the Greek Orthodox Church, Jerome Kotsonis, who, while assistant to his predecessor, Archbishop Spiridon, interpreted me when I addressed groups of the Greek Orthodox Church in Athens in 1961.

To Dr. A. Edwin Keigwin who prayed that I would be ordained by the Presbyterian Church. To Dr. Alfred Grant Walton who proposed me for ordination by the Congregational Churches. Also to the Episcopal Bishops, George Craig Stewart of Chicago, James Edward Freeman of Washington, Milmore Stires of Long Island, Horace B. Donegan of New York and Clinton Simon Quinn of Houston, Texas, who, through the years, were the friends of my ministry. Lastly to my son-in-law, the Rev. Claxton Monro, in whose church, St. Stephen's Episcopal, Houston, Texas, I preached several times.

I have undertaken this writing with deep humility. Others have written more comprehensively on the subject. However, "unto whom much is given, of him much shall be required."[7] Hence . . . this book.

Finally, I cannot finish this preface without expressing my deepest gratitude to a beloved friend. She wishes to remain anonymous, but without her constant encouragement, understanding, devotion, and skillful assistance, this book could never have been written.

The Reverend Victoria Booth Demarest today. —*Photo by Eleanor Lehner*

A Sacred Arts International Photograph

God, Woman
& Ministry

P. Xii
most major
protestant agreed
Ordain women.

11 women Epis.
priest - July 19, 1974.
in Philly.

Xiii → grandmother
Catherine Mumford
Booth.
She was ordained
1949

XIV - not speaking
as feminist - 1st
priority of a
Christian -

?.28 - 1st person
publicly proclaimed
coming of Jesus -
Anna - 1st -
resurrection Mary

p. 29 - Women at
well
---
p. 33
Martha/Mary
---
p. 35
Cross & Resurrection
---
p. 36
1st to preach Complete
gospel — Mary Magdalene
---
p. 38 -
Pentecost

p. 40 Catherine Booth
preaching Testimony

p. 44-45
Women & the
Early Church -
Phoebe, Junia,
Lydia
---
p. 48. - Tertullias -
Jerome historian

Chapter One

GOD IS NOT MAN

Though the Scriptures refer to God in masculine terms, *God is Not Man.*

"God is a Spirit," said Jesus to the Samaritan woman. "They that worship him must worship him in spirit and in truth."[1]

"God is a Spirit."

There is no sex in spirit. God is neither male nor female.

Nevertheless, God is a *Being* — not a *Thing* — and the Scriptures attribute to him both masculine and feminine characteristics.

WOMAN in CREATION

To make man "in his own image," both "male and female created he them."[2]

Not merely *Man* . . .

Not merely *Woman* . . .

But *Human Beings* — meaning both. Without woman God's image of himself was incomplete.

In God we see feminine attributes. In the beginning the Holy Spirit brooded over the waters.[3] Isaiah spoke of

him as a mother.[4] As poet James Weldon Johnson en-
visioned it:

> This great God,
> Like a mammy bending over her baby,
> Kneeled down in the dust
> Toiling over a lump of clay
> Till he shaped it in his own image.
> Then into it he blew the breath of life,
> And man became a living soul.[5]

The Apostle John identified Jesus with the Word —
Logos — the Wisdom personified as female in the Book of
Proverbs.[6]

Christ was the express image of God's person. In
him dwelt "all the fullness of the Godhead bodily."[7] As
such, he exemplified not only courage, strength, boldness,
fearlessness (generally regarded as masculine traits), but
also love, gentleness, compassion, and the mother instinct
(accepted as feminine traits). What could be more feminine
than his comment, How often I would have gathered you
as a hen gathers her chickens under her wings![8] Although
we think of God as our "Father," we think of him also as
our "Comforter" — a mother's role. Jesus called the Holy
Spirit by that name.[9]

In his three parables which reveal the love of God for
sinners, Jesus likened the grace of God not only to that of
a shepherd seeking a lost sheep, or of a father forgiving a
repentant prodigal son — but also to that of a woman seeking and finding a lost coin.[10]

God speaks of himself as fulfilling the roles of both
a mother and a father.[11] In the Godhead we may see the
human family represented — God the Father, the Holy
Spirit the Mother, Jesus Christ the Son — *One God,*

Father, Son and Holy Spirit. We might say that, on the day of Pentecost, the Church was born from the womb of the Holy Spirit.

A CHILD'S VIEW

Describing God as possessing both masculine and feminine characteristics reminds me of an incident in my childhood. I was second in a family of ten children, five boys and five girls, and was immediately followed by four brothers — Herbert, Augustin, William, and Eric. Before going to sleep each night we always said our prayers kneeling beside our beds. Mother taught us to talk to God as naturally as we talked to her.

One night we heard four-year-old Willie praying, "Dear Jesus, you are the most wonderful woman. . . "

"Willie!" Augustin interrupted. "Jesus is not a woman. He is a man."

"Augustin," Willie answered with exaggerated patience. "I am praying! . . . Oh Jesus, you are the most wonderful woman . . ."

By that time Mother had entered the room. She lifted Willie to her lap and gently inquired, "Darling, why do you think that Jesus is a woman?"

"Because," said Willie, "he is so tender towards us."

"Out of the mouths of babes . . .!"[12]

A POET'S VIEW

To pass from the innate wisdom of a child to the inspired wisdom of a poet, it has been said of John Milton's "Paradise Lost" and "Paradise Regained" that "his poetic imagination soared far above his conscious theorizing" in his efforts to make clear that "God is literally neither male nor female." According to Virginia Ramey Mollenkort,

"Milton, as much as any poet or mystic and far more than most, freed himself from the tendency to anthropomorphize God. *His metaphors challenge us to do the same* to abandon our traditionally sexist assumption about the nature of God and to put into practice Paul's liberating vision of a classless, non-sexist Christian society."[13]

THE INTERMINGLING OF THE SEXES

"Male and female created he them." In this context it is interesting to note that characteristics generally called feminine and masculine are in fact mingled and present in both sexes. A man is no less masculine if he has an element of tenderness in his nature or is more dependent emotionally than a woman. And a woman is no less feminine if she has the strong personality of a leader. These mixed sex elements may often be observed in the great artists, scientists, leaders, and saints of history.

It is related that Christ appeared to Catherine of Sienna, the 14th-century saint, when she was only nineteen.

"Do *manfully,* my daughter," he said to her. "Being armed with the fortitude of the Faith you will happily overcome all your adversaries."

Apprehensively the young nun demurred. "Who am I, a woman, to go into public service?"

"The word *impossible* belongs not to God," came the answer. "Am I not I he who created the human race, who formed both man and woman. *I pour out the favor of my Spirit on whom I will.* Go forth without fear, in spite of reproach. I have a mission for you to fulfill."

Catherine did as she was told, and eventually passed along the advice she had received: "Rise up *manfully,* sweet sister," she admonished Queen Joan of Naples. "For love's sake lift up the standard of the most holy cross in your heart."[14]

When I was in my teens I read and reread Mark Twain's biography of Joan of Arc.[15] I loved that book. It challenged me to brave endeavor and sacrifice. Next to my Bible it was the book which most compellingly inspired me to dedicate my life to the service of God. I was impressed not only by Joan's reverence, faith, and courage, but also by her genuine femininity — a beautiful, womanly quality that elicited from her soldier-followers an allegiance both passionate and reverent, exemplifying the most perfect type of leadership.

At the same time, in contrast to the French Dauphin, who was such a weakling, Joan was a true and great general. "In all of our recorded history, she holds the distinction of being *the only person of either sex* who, at the age of seventeen, served as the supreme commander of the military forces of a nation." Her soldiers loved her, respected her, believed in her, and followed her without hesitation even into death. Has any male general ever inspired greater devotion?

In the service of God both men and women are called upon to consecrate to him *all* the qualities, characteristics, and gifts inherent in their natures. To that end the promises of God and his saving grace are given to both men and women *equally*. The masculine gender in the Scriptures, with few exceptions, is used in the generic (universal) sense. There is certainly no differentiation of masculine and feminine in "the fruit of the Spirit." Both men and women are heirs of grace and called on to manifest in their lives "love, joy, peace, longsuffering, gentleness, goodness, faith, meekness, temperance."[16] Both men and women are called upon to "put on the whole armor of God"[17] and to be "good soldiers of Jesus Christ." [18]

EQUALITY IN GOD

At creation, woman, like man, was made in the image of God and "crowned with glory and honor,"[19] and to both was given dominion over every living thing and over all the earth.[20] At creation, woman was given the same honors, privileges, and responsibilities as man. At creation, because God intended companionship between man and woman, he made both of them moral and intelligent beings, alike in their dignity and worth.

In Christ both man and woman are redeemed from the results of "the fall" — the results of sin. The needs, rights, and responsibilities of both are equally worthy of recognition and respect. In Christ man and woman are *One.*[21]

"Never 'til woman is estimated and educated as man's equal — the literal She-Man of the Hebrew — will the foundation of human influence become pure or the bias of mind noble and lofty,"[22] wrote Catherine Booth.

"Christ transcends maleness, as Paul taught," wrote the Rev. Adiel J. Moncrief.[23] "He was the full embodiment of humanity, male and female, of all races and kinds, and he is both the symbol and source of all regenerate mankind. The theological and dogmatic devices which men have worked out are now forced to yield to the pressure of new life which is the fruit of the gospel."

Since both man and woman are represented in God, he ministers to both equally, and he calls both equally to minister to him and for him.

Chapter Two

JESUS AND WOMAN

From his birth to his death and resurrection women played a significant role in the life of Jesus, and it is evident that his attitude toward them was one of sensitivity and respect.

AT HIS BIRTH

The first woman to be mentioned in connection with Jesus is, of course, his mother *Mary.* "You are blessed among women," said the angel to her in his annunciation. "You have found favor with God."[1]

The eternal God "whose eyes run up and down the earth seeking those whose hearts are perfect toward him," passed by the great, the queens, the learned among women, and chose this maiden of low estate — whom tradition tells us was only about sixteen — to be the mother of his Son. In doing so he was true to his character and mode of action, as described by Paul in a letter to the Church in Corinth: "Not many wise men . . . not many mighty . . . not many noble are called; but God hath chosen the foolish things . . . the weak things . . . the base things . . . the things which are despised . . . and the things which are not, to bring to nought the things that are."[2]

Heaven must have waited breathlessly for this maiden's answer to the challenge implicit in the annunciation . . . and rejoiced when it came, beautiful in its humility and simplicity. "Behold the handmaid of the Lord, be it done to me according to your word."[3]

Without Mary's consent, the Incarnation could not have taken place. She was not a dead, passive tool in the hand of God. She was a living, loving participant in his plan. Mary's faith, courage, and selflessness made the Incarnation possible, and these qualities mark her life from the birth of Jesus through his death on the Cross.

Mary was not the meek, unobtrusive, insignificant person many scholars have described! She had the courage to undertake a long journey, alone, to share her divine secret with her cousin Elizabeth. Her song, the "Magnificat,"[4] one of the great treasures of the church, reveals her intelligence, her deep spiritual understanding of the scriptures, and her strong, joyous faith. It is truly a sermon.

It was the apostle Paul who wrote that the son of God, made of a woman, would redeem those who were under the law.[5] This redemption included woman, who certainly was in bondage to the law. Through that redemption she was restored to the place she originally occupied in God's plan — a "helpmate for man,"[6] worthy of him and equal to him.

It was Mary, not Joseph, who rebuked Jesus, when he was twelve years old, for alarming them by remaining behind in Jerusalem. And it was to Mary that Jesus gave his revealing answer, "I must be about my Father's business."[7]

Many times in her life Mary must have been tempted to speak — to defend her own reputation or to defend her son when he was being maligned. But she demonstrated her great courage by remaining silent. Only on one occasion did she publicly express herself with authority — at the marriage in Cana when the wine gave out. Proud of her son and certain that he could find a way to solve the problem, she risked an indirect request for a miracle. She pointed out to Jesus, "They have no wine."[8]

Jesus understood what she was asking, and in his answer he reminded her that she must not attempt to influence him. Your concern, Mother, is not mine, he replied. "My hour has not yet come."[9]

Mary accepted the rebuke, but her faith in him did not waver. May it have been her steadfast faith and her selfless yielding to his authority that prompted Jesus, shortly afterwards, to reward his magnificent mother with a miracle?

Whatever the reason, Mary was ready for it when it came. Her response was to deliver one of the greatest — and yet briefest — sermons ever preached. "Whatever he tells you to do, *do it*,"[10] she advised the servants when Jesus told them to fill the wine vessels with water.

Don't question! Don't discuss it with wife, husband, or neighbor! Don't hesitate! Don't seek to understand! Just "do it."

And the water was changed into wine. A woman's faith, courage, and selflessness inspired the first miracle of Jesus.

Jesus never forgot Mary. Not even his excruciating suffering on the Cross could blot her out of his mind. In his supreme agony he was conscious of her presence at the foot of his Cross, and he made certain that she would be cared for by entrusting her to his beloved disciple John. As for Mary, with the agonizing crucifixion and joyful resurrection behind her, she took her place with the apostles and the other women in the upper room on the day of Pentecost. And she, along with the others, received the Holy Spirit — and *prophesied.*[11]

It is significant that the first person who publicly proclaimed the coming of Jesus was a woman, *Anna*. And the first person to proclaim his resurrection was also a woman, *Mary Magdalene*.

Anna, the prophetess, was an 84-year-old woman who lived in the temple, and served God night and day with fastings and prayer.[12] One day she came into the temple just as Simeon, with the child Jesus in his arms, uttered the prophetic words: ". . . mine eyes have seen Thy salvation." And immediately she went out to "speak of him to all the people in Jerusalem that looked for redemption." Was this not preaching?

AS MOTHERS

Jesus understood and respected mothers. When preachers quote his invitation, Let the little ones come unto me for such is the kingdom of heaven, I have never heard them mention the mothers who brought those children. How hurt those mothers must have been when the male disciples turned them away, assuming that the Master could not be bothered with a pack of women and their babies! (A typical attitude toward women.) Some of those mothers must have come a long distance, carrying or leading their children, because they were eager for their little ones to receive a blessing from Jesus. The children would not have known, and the disciples certainly never thought of it. But Jesus understood. And how it must have gladdened the hearts of those mothers to hear him rebuke the disciples and invite the children to be brought to him.[13]

On another occasion Jesus demonstrated his understanding of a mother's heart when her son's body was being carried on a bier through the gate of the city of Nain. The mother was a widow and he was her only son. These few words say much. Being a widow she must have poured

all her love on this only son, and he must have provided
for her. Now she was alone! Where would she go? What
could she do? She was weeping as she followed the bier.
Jesus happened along and "his heart went out to her."
Tenderly he said, "Do not weep any more." Touching the
bier, he told the young man to arise. And he that was dead
sat up and began to speak. As the scriptures describe it,
"Jesus gave him back to his mother."[14] Can we conceive
of her joy?

AS PERSONS

Jesus never indicated that he considered women in-
ferior to men. In fact, his behavior suggested that he
respected them as equals. At the well in Sychar in Samaria,
for example, the disciples were astonished to find him
talking to a Samaritan woman. It was considered improper
to be seen conversing with even a Jewish woman — let
alone a Samaritan, with whom the Jews had no dealings
whatever.[15]

Yet this Samaritan woman shares with Nicodemus[16]
the distinction of having called forth two of the most significant messages of Jesus. To this woman, a despised
Samaritan, he revealed for the first time that he was Christ,
the Messiah. "I that speak unto thee am he."[17]

Is it any wonder that, in her excitement, the woman
dropped her water pot, forgot her daily chores, and
hurried to the city to tell forth this eternally significant
news? She did not hesitate. She did not ask him to explain.
She accepted his words and proclaimed them to the people.
Hers was an act of prophetic preaching, and it was in
response to her words that the people went to hear Jesus
and implored him to remain with them. To the woman,
they said, We believe in him *not only because of your*

words but also because we have heard him ourselves and know that this is indeed the Christ, the Savior of the world.[18]

There are many recorded incidents demonstrating that Jesus understood women and was sensitive to their feelings. When the Pharisees dragged a young woman into his presence, announcing that she had been taken in adultery, he knew that they wanted to trap him into condemning her to be stoned to death according to the law of Moses. But his first concern was for the woman. He did not even look at her, knowing that this would intensify her suffering and humiliation. Instead, he said to the Pharisees, "That one of you who is faultless shall throw the first stone."

Chagrinned, the Pharisees retreated like whipped dogs. Only when left alone with the woman did Jesus turn to her and utter these words of forgiveness and deliverance: "Neither do I condemn thee, go and sin no more."[19]

Would it not be natural for this woman to want to share with others her gratitude, her worship of this uniquely forgiving being? Who would wish to deny her the right?

Jesus always accepted woman as a person even if her past was disreputable. Another example is the story of the "woman of the city who was a sinner."[20]

In those days a feast for an honored guest was more or less a public affair. People of the town gathered to look in on the festivities. On this occasion it is evident that the Pharisee host had invited Jesus not because of his admiration for him or respect for his teachings, but merely for the sake of the prestige he could gain by entertaining a popular figure.

Jesus was fully aware of his attitude, which was so in contrast to that of the woman who burst into the feast uninvited. Her actions reveal that she must have heard

Jesus speak on some previous occasion. She must have waited for an opportunity to let him know what his words had meant to her. At last he was within reach. But — in the house of a Pharisee! She knew the law. As a prostitute she could be stoned. Nevertheless, even if she lost her life, she must go to him. When, at last, she fell at his feet, only her tears and kisses could speak for her.

Aware of the Pharisee's unspoken fury and disgust, Jesus made this woman the means for delivering one of his most significant messages. He rebuked his host for his uncouth manners, while, at the same time, making the woman *a partner in his ministry.*

When I entered your house, he told the Pharisee, you omitted all of the courtesies to which I was entitled — the washing of my feet by a slave, the kiss of welcome, the annointing of my head with oil. But this woman's tears of repentance have washed my feet. Her kisses have demonstrated the depth of her devotion and gratitude. She was willing to sacrifice not only her fortune — to buy the alabaster box of precious ointment with which she has annointed my feet — but also her life. She loves much and is therefore forgiven much.

Then Jesus uttered to the woman these redeeming words: "Thy sins are forgiven . . . Thy faith hath saved thee, go in peace."

It is to be noted that Jesus used a woman, a repentant prostitute, to teach a man, a religious leader, a lesson in good manners, in repentance and in love.

Because of her love and faith, this woman has been taken to the heart of the whole church as the Mary Magdalene, whose name is first mentioned in the very next chapter of the Gospel story and who, we are told, was delivered of "seven devils" and became one of the women who ministered to Jesus. Those women included not only the rich and socially and politically prominent, such as

Joanna, the wife of Herod's steward, but also the poor and those with a morally disreputable past, showing that from the very beginning there was no distinction either of background or wealth, among the disciples of Jesus. It is to be noted that the Bible mentions no other monetary contributions to Jesus and his apostles except those of women.

AS EXAMPLES

Jesus liked to point out examples of prayer, courage, humility, faith, and sacrifice in the behavior of women. To illustrate the need for perseverance in prayer, he described a widow who kept imploring a magistrate for protection from a wicked man who was trying to ruin her. Although the magistrate boasted that he feared neither God nor his fellow man, he finally granted the widow's plea to avoid her continual requests. [21]

Jesus warned that the Queen of the South would rise up in the judgment and condemn the men of this generation; for "she came from the utmost parts of the earth to hear the wisdom of Solomon; and a greater than Solomon is here." [22]

Jesus was impressed by a woman who begged him to deliver her daughter from a devil. But first, to test her faith, he turned her down. Her response was to throw herself at his feet, declaring that, like a dog, she would gladly eat the crumbs from her Master's table. "Oh, woman, great is thy faith," he exclaimed. "Be it unto thee as thou wilt" [23]

Another example of the efficacy of faith was the woman who, for twelve years, spent all her money on doctors who could not heal her constant hemorrhage. According to Jewish law, she was unclean and forbidden to approach Jesus. But she secretly touched his cloak, saying to herself, "If I can only touch his clothes, I will be well." Aware that healing power had gone out of him, Jesus asked, "Who touched me?" "You are being jostled by many," the people exclaimed. Frightened, the woman fell at his feet and confessed. Instead of a rebuke, she heard the beautiful word, "Daughter." And then Jesus told her, "Be of good comfort. Thy faith has made thee whole. Go in peace." [24]

Jesus also called attention to the generosity of a poor widow. He had seen her give "more than all those who cast their money into the treasury," he said. For "they all contributed out of their abundance; but she out of her poverty has given all that she possessed."[25]

AS FRIENDS

The special friendship which Jesus seemed to feel for Martha and Mary of Bethany gives us an illustration of the emphasis he placed on the spiritual development of women.

Jesus was a frequent guest in their home in Bethany. It was the one place where he could relax among those who loved and understood him — Martha, who attended to his material needs; Mary, who loved him deeply; and their brother Lazarus. He could appreciate their need for practical housekeeping skills. But he considered their spiritual education even more important. We are told that Martha complained to Jesus that Mary left her to do all of the housework while she sat at his feet listening to his teachings. Martha thought that Jesus should rebuke Mary for this. But Jesus replied that Mary had chosen the better part and that it should not be taken away from her. [26]

Would Jesus have objected if Mary had decided to pass on to others the spiritual truths which he was so eager to impart and she to learn? Would he have said, "No, my dear, that is only man's work"?

That Jesus may have felt a special love for Mary is suggested in the story of the raising of Lazarus from the dead.[27]

When Jesus arrived at their home, fully aware that Lazarus was dead, Martha greeted him with the words, "Lord, if you had been here my brother would not have died." And Jesus replied, "I am the resurrection and the life," and promised to raise Lazarus from the dead.

But when Mary appeared, fell at his feet, and repeated Martha's words, Jesus could not speak. Instead, he groaned in spirit and wept. Martha drew words. Mary drew tears.

I believe that Jesus found in Mary, and also in John, called "the disciple whom Jesus loved," a deep understanding of him and of his mission, which confirms that a woman, as well as a man, can enter into the deeper things of God.

(However, it should not be forgotten that it was *Martha* who, on this occasion, declared Jesus to be Christ, the son of God. One man made this declaration, the apostle Peter,[28] and two women — the Samaritan, as already pointed out, and Martha.)

Mary revealed a unique appreciation of the meaning of the life and death of Jesus. She had prophetic insight. This was manifested when Jesus visited their home for the last time, six days before the Passover.

At that time, Mary poured a very costly ointment on his head as he sat at meat. The fragrance filled the house. The disciples, indignant, exclaimed, "To what purpose is this waste? The ointment might have been sold for much and the money given to the poor."

But Jesus rebuked them with the words: "Why trouble her? Let her alone. You have the poor always with you, and whenever you will you can do them good, but me you have not always. She has done what she could and has anointed my body beforehand for my burial." And he added, "Truly wheresoever this Gospel shall be preached throughout the world, what this woman has done shall be spoken of as a memorial of her."[29]

AT HIS CROSS AND RESURRECTION

Let us remember that:
Only women followed Jesus on the Via Dolorosa. . .
Only women wailed and lamented over him. . .
Only women, with the exception of John, stood by his Cross. . .[30]
Only women were at his grave to discover his resurrection.[31]

The men disciples had fled,[32] except John, who ran after him, naked, leaving his garment in the hands of a soldier, and Peter who followed afar off.

In the courtyard of the place where Jesus was being tried, Peter denied him three times with curses and with oaths. The cock crew. And Peter remembered that Jesus had foretold his denial! And when Jesus was being led past the courtyard he looked at him and we read that Peter went out and wept bitterly.[33]

No woman fled.
No woman denied him.
No woman left him alone to suffer.

Jesus was conscious of the presence of the women and of their love and pity and it must have brought comfort to him. But it brought sorrow as well.

On the way to Golgotha, falling repeatedly under the burden of the Cross, his body bruised and bleeding from the scourging, he became conscious of the loud weeping of the women. Ignoring his own suffering, he thought of the greater sorrows ahead for them. "Daughters of Jerusalem," he called to them, "weep not for me, but for yourselves and for your children."[34]

In speaking of women in the life of Jesus, we should not forget the wife of Pilate.[35] She may have been a secret disciple. At any rate, she must have heard Jesus speak and been greatly affected, even to the extent that she dreamed about him. What she dreamed we do not know, but evidently it caused her great suffering. It must have been powerful, or she would not have had the courage to send a message to Pilate while he was in court — a message imploring him not to condemn Jesus to death. In fact, she urged Pilate not to harm this righteous and innocent man. This woman had greater spiritual insight than her husband.

As an illustration that God expected women to preach, one of our Savior's final acts on earth was to send Mary Magdalene to announce — to his own apostles — his resurrection and coming ascension.[36] *She was really the first to preach the complete Gospel,* which Paul defines as being the "good news" that Jesus was born, was crucified for our sins, and that he rose again for our justification. [37] *The Gospel was not completed* until Jesus was risen from the dead, as announced by Mary Magdalene.

We are told that the disciples did not believe her or the other women who corroborated her news — that they dismissed her message as "idle tales." Could this have been because the messenger was not a man? It was difficult for them to accept the fact that Jesus would bestow such an honor on a woman. When Jesus appeared to them later he rebuked them for their unbelief.[38]

On an earlier occasion Jesus had shown his respect for feminine discipleship by declaring, "Whoever shall do the will of My Father which is in heaven, the same is my brother, and sister, and mother."[39]

Clearly Jesus appreciated women ... respected

women . . . encouraged women to learn and to preach
. . . and never overlooked an opportunity to prepare men
to receive the spiritual ministry of women.

Chapter Three

THE DIVINE EMANCIPATION
OF WOMAN

PENTECOST

The most significant commission to women as prophets occurred on the day of Pentecost, the birthday of the church, when 120 men *and women,* including Mary, the Mother of Jesus, were assembled. All of them were waiting for the baptism of the Holy Spirit, as Jesus had instructed them to do. And when the Holy Spirit descended all of them began to prophesy.[1]

The people who were watching started mocking, accusing them of being drunk. This evoked Peter's great declaration which signified the Holy Spirit's emancipation of women and settled once and for all the question of woman's equal right, with man, to preach the Gospel.

Quoting the prophet Joel, Peter said, "In the last days I will pour out of my spirit upon all flesh: and your sons and *your daughters* shall prophesy . . . on my servants and on my *handmaidens* I will pour out in those days of my spirit: and *they shall prophesy.*"[2]

The word *prophesy* in the Scriptures has two meanings: 1) to foretell the future, and 2) to tell forth the wonderful works of God. The latter is preaching.

On the day of Pentecost, the disciples did not *foretell.* They *told forth,* or preached. And, miraculously, *every man heard them speak in his own language.*[3]

If the baptism of the Holy Spirit and the gift of prophecy had been intended for men alone, if the women had been sent home and only the men had remained, there would have been a false note in Peter's declaration, which was the founding block of the church. Would this not have done an injustice to the Holy Spirit?

Throughout the New Testament God is spoken of sometimes as *Father,* sometimes as *Christ,* and sometimes as *Holy Spirit.* The word *Trinity* is nowhere found in the scriptures. It was coined by the Church to define and clarify the faith and experience of Christian believers. They knew God as *Father* — they were born again as his children.[4] They knew God as *Savior* — in the Person of Christ. And they knew God as *Holy Spirit* — through his divine power in their lives.

Nature gives us a beautiful illustration of the triune God — light which is *one* but has *three* distinct properties! The actinic which cannot be seen — "No man has seen God at any time."[5] The luminiferous which is light as we know it — Jesus said, "I am the light of the world."[6] The calorific which is not seen but felt — *the heat, the fire, the passion* — *the Holy Spirit.*

On the day of Pentecost flames of fire (symbolical of the Holy Spirit) were seen to light on the heads of all the disciples, men and women. This fire of God is the fire of love ("God is love") without which the many gifts of the Spirit, including that of prophetic preaching, Paul tells us are without value.[7] On that day the fire of LOVE — for God, for each other, for all men, even for their enemies — fell on the disciples, women as well as men. (The love of God is shed abroad in our hearts by the Holy Spirit.)[8] And it is noteworthy that this pentecostal experience is conjoined in the gospel of Luke and in the Acts of the Apostles with the commission *to preach the Gospel to the ends of the earth.*[9] That commission was given to representatives of the *whole church,* and they included women.

DIVINE COMPULSION — CATHERINE BOOTH

Whenever the fire falls on either man or woman, it creates a compulsion which must not be disobeyed. Since the day of Pentecost, many women have clearly demonstrated, by their actions, that they have received this enduement of power, but few have described the actual occurrence.

Obedience to this compulsion, by both men and women, has resulted in good for humanity that cannot be computed. One illustration of this was the Salvation Army, which William Booth could never have created without his wife's unfailing inspiration and assistance. In her own words Catherine Booth has recorded her experience in which the Holy Spirit compelled her to begin her preaching career.

I was in the minister's pew with my eldest boy Bramwell, then four years old. (See Appendix B) I felt depressed in mind, and was not expecting anything, but as the testimonies proceeded *I felt the Holy Spirit come upon me.* You alone who have experienced it can tell what this means. It cannot be described. I felt it to the extremity of my hands and feet. It seemed as if a voice said to me, "Now if you were to testify, you know I would bless it to your own soul, as well as to the people!" I said to my heart, "Yes, Lord, I believe you would, but I cannot do it." I had forgotten my vow. (She had promised the Lord that she would obey him at all cost. See Appendix C) I felt as though I would sooner die than speak. Then the devil said, "Besides, you are not prepared. You will look like a fool and will have nothing to say." He overreached himself for once. "Ah!" I said, "this is just the point. I have never yet been willing to be a fool for Christ. Now I will be one!" I rose from my seat and walked down the aisle. My dear husband was just going to conclude his meeting. He thought something had happened to

Catherine Mumford Booth
1829-1890
"Mother of the Salvation Army"

me, so did the people. *They knew my timid, bashful nature.* He stepped down and asked me, "What is the matter, my dear?" I replied, "I want to say a word." He was so surprised that he could only say, "My dear wife wishes to speak," and sat down. I said: "I dare say many of you have been looking upon me as a very devout woman, *but I have been disobeying God,* and thus have brought darkness and leanness into my soul. I promised the Lord to do so no longer. Henceforth I will be obedient to the Holy vision." [10]

Catherine had scarcely resumed her seat when William, with his typical "eye to business," the Lord's business, announced: "My wife will preach tonight." Her servant, who was at the meeting, went home and danced around the kitchen table with delight, calling out to the nurse, "The mistress has spoken! The mistress has spoken!" And little did Catherine think that her two-year-old daughter (my mother), sleeping peacefully upstairs, would become one of the greatest women preachers in history, turning thousands to God in France, Switzerland, Holland, Belgium, Canada, and the United States.

That night the chapel was crowded to the doors. The people even sat on the window sills. *And it was the anniversary of Pentecost!* [11]

"So began the most wonderful example of Female Ministry on record," wrote the Rev. Maude Royden, who was, herself, a noted British preacher in the 1920s.

In describing Catherine Booth, Miss Royden commented:

> For twenty-five years . . . although virtually an invalid, and not knowing what it was to pass a day free from pain, although mother of four more children born in the very midst of her public activities, although harassed with the financial and domestic cares of her large household, she preached continu-

ously to overflowing congregations in every part of the country, signs and wonders following. The physical cost was prodigious. Scores of times this "gladiator soul" sallied from her sick bed to face the eager waiting crowds who hung upon her lips, and no sooner had she finished than she hurried back to it, utterly prostrated by the effort . . . Above all, she was the *"Mother of the Salvation Army."* [12]

His wife encouraged and assisted William Booth in founding a new religious movement which spread in a single generation over the whole surface of the globe. When she was thirty (in 1859), she wrote her pamphlet in defense of women's ministry in a single week, working from seven every morning until eleven every night. Her example, her many writings, preachings, and teachings, led to the opening of the mouths of thousands of women for the preaching of the Gospel.

From her earliest childhood Catherine Booth had been preparing for this. Before she was twelve years old she had read the complete Bible eight times. (She was better versed in the Scriptures than her husband.) From her infancy her Godly mother had encouraged her along spiritual lines, and at the age of fifteen, after experiencing several days of spiritual agony and striving, she received the assurance that she was a child of God and that her sins were forgiven.

Her first writing on the subject of equality of woman and her right to preach the Gospel was a letter to her pastor, which she wrote when she was seventeen years old. Before ever meeting William Booth, she described to God in prayer the kind of man she wanted to marry, and told God emphatically that she would never have a wicked child. Her prayer was answered in every detail. But she would not marry William until he accepted her convictions regarding women. From the day they met she was his inspiration. At his request, she prepared outlines for many of his sermons. She assisted him in all his evangelistic endeavors. But, though she believed firmly in women's right to preach and had written several papers on the subject, she steadfastly refused to preach herself — until that day in 1860 *when she obeyed the Holy Spirit.* It is estimated that before she died in 1890, she had preached to one million people. Catherine Booth had obeyèd the Holy Spirit. More than fifty thousand passed by her coffin in Congress Hall and in the Olympia. More than thirty-six thousand attended the funeral service.

W. T. Stead wrote that, "Judging from such data as are now available it seems probable that the future historian may record that no woman of the Victorian era—except it be the monarch who gives her name to the epoch — has done more to help in the making of modern England."[13]

WOMAN AND THE EARLY CHURCH

The Pentecostal experience which compelled Catherine Booth to preach — her commission from the Holy Spirit — reminds us that God the Holy Spirit ruled the early church. "The Acts of the Apostles" might well have been called "The Acts of the Holy Spirit"; for we read that the Holy Spirit "spake" . . . "forbade" . . . "commanded" . . . "sent" . . . "restrained." Every decision, every act, every mission in the early church was taken or made under the direction, by the command, or through the inspiration of the Holy Spirit. And many women were mentioned, both in the Acts of the Apostles and in Paul's letters to the churches, as having been *agents of the Holy Spirit.*

Four unmarried daughters[14] of Philip were evangelists. "They preached God's word."

Phoebe[15] was "minister of the Church of Cench-
rea." The Greek word, *diakonon*, translated *minister* in the
case of Paul, is translated *servant* or *deaconess* in the case
of Phoebe, indicating sex bias on the part of male translators. (The New Testament in Modern English restores her
title of *minister.*) She was also an administrator. The word,
prostatis, translated *helper* in the authorized version,
actually means one who rules, superintends. It is translated
overseer in The New Testament in Modern English.

Junia[16] was "of note among the Apostles." *Junia*
was a feminine name, but some translators rendered it in
the masculine, *Junius.* Paul wrote that Junia became a
Christian before he did. She was referred to as an apostle
in the fourth century by no less an authority than Chrisos-
tom, Bishop of Constantinople.

Lydia[17] was minister of the first church in Europe,
which met in her home.

The *mother of John Mark*, and *Chloe*, the latter a
prominent Greek woman, both had churches in their
homes.[18]

Damaris,[19] converted by Paul, was a Greek woman
of "honorable estate." She is mentioned in connection
with Dionysius, a judge, and probably was one of the
Hetairai, a highly intellectual class of women philosophers
and stateswomen.

Lois and *Eunice*[20] are praised in Paul's letter to the
young Timothy, his "beloved child in the Gospel." He
wrote, "I long to see you and have the perfect happiness of
being reminded of your genuine faith, *a faith that lived
permanently in the heart of your grandmother Lois and in
your mother Eunice.*"

Euodias and Syntyche were also active in church
ministry. They were typically feminine since Paul advised
them to get along with each other![21]

In his letter to the Romans, Paul saluted *Mary*,

"who bestowed so much labor upon us"; the *Mother of Rufus,* "who has been a mother to me"; *Julia* and *"the sister of Nereus";* and *"Tryphena* and *Tryphosa";*[22] and in his letter to the Colossians he mentioned *Nympha* and the church in her house. In the *King James* version, whose translators did not have access to the earliest manuscripts, this passage refers to "Nymphas, and the church which is in *his* house," as does *The Living Bible.* But the five other translations I consulted all refer to Nympha as a woman.[23]

The frequent references to churches in the homes of these women remind us of the simplicity of early church gatherings, many of which took place in private houses.

An early epistle not included in the New Testament, known as the *Acts of Paul and Thecla,* affirms that she too was a female apostle. Manuscripts still exist in Greek, Latin, Syriac, Arabic, and Slavonic.[24]

Another woman, *Dorcas,* ministered to the church in practical, loving ways. Her death caused such widespread grief that Peter was summoned to the house where her body was lying. And Peter prayed. And Dorcus returned to life. Commenting about this miracle, Professor W. G. Elmslie suggested that God singled out this gentle, kindly woman in order to set a mark of honor upon the love she manifested. This was God's way of teaching that death could be conquered not by preaching or by miracleworking, or by gifts, or by conspicuous deeds — but only by love.[25]

One of the most prominent early Christians was *Priscilla,*[26] the wife of Aquila.

Four times out of six, in the New Testament, Priscilla is saluted ahead of her husband. Such recognition for a woman was almost unheard of. The only explanation would seem to be that she held an outstanding position in the church. Scholars believe that it was she, even more than Aquila, who "expounded the scriptures" to the orator and scholar Apollos — himself "mighty in the scriptures."[27]

Paul called Priscilla and Aquila his "helpers . . . who have for my life laid down their own necks: upon whom not only I give thanks, but also all the churches of the Gentiles."[28]

PRISCILLA — AND THE EPISTLE TO THE HEBREWS

The renowned theologian, Adolph V. Harnack was the first to suggest that, in his opinion, Priscilla probably authored the Epistle to the Hebrews. (See Appendix D) I was overjoyed when this was called to my attention by my brother-in-law, Dr. James Strachan, professor at the University of Edinburth and author of *The Maréchale.*

Such unusual recognition of a woman by so eminent an authority certainly deserves serious attention. Several other scholars — including such names as Moulton, Schiele, Peak, and Rendel Harris — have concurred with him.

Dr. Lee Anna Starr listed thirteen points for testing Harnack's hypothesis (see Appendix E), and devoted eleven pages of her book, *The Bible Status of Women,* to demonstrating (as a result of meticulous research) that none of the men proposed as the possible author by various commentators — not even the Apostle Paul — meet the requirements of these tests. Only Priscilla meets them all!

In my own viewpoint, the fact that the author's name is omitted provides the most convincing evidence favoring a conclusion that a woman wrote this epistle. This seems the only plausible reason for the author's anonymity.

This argument was supported by A. C. Headlam[27] who wrote: "The authorship of Priscilla will explain why the writing is now anonymous. The church of the Second Century objected very strongly to the prominent position of women in the Apostolic Age. This had caused the gradual modification of various passages in the Acts and the desire to separate this work from the name of Priscilla."

My sense of justice revolts against presuming that a man wrote this epistle when it might have been written by a woman. May I suggest that future editions of the Bible list the names of *all* possible authors — including Priscilla?

Priscilla was a preacher as well as a teacher. Tertullias wrote, "By the holy Prisca the Gospel is preached."[29] A catacomb and a church in Rome are named in her honor.

There were other women preachers and teachers in the early days of the Church. The historian Jerome[29] (350-390 A.D.) mentioned several, among them *Marcella*, who publicly preached the Gospel in Rome. He paid her this tribute: "All that I learnt with great study and long meditation, the blessed Marcella easily learnt also, but with great facility, and without giving up any of her other occupations, or neglecting any of her pursuits. . . .Rome became Jerusalem under the influence of Marcella." Difficulties in translation were submitted to her, he added, and "always we had reason to admire the correctness of her decision."

Jerome wrote also about *Paula* (Vidua), a famous Hebrew scholar. He confessed that he referred to her the most difficult portion of his commentary on Ezekiel.

Jerome lauded *Demetria* as a "prodigy of sanctity." And he called *Febrolas* "The Wonder of the Ages."

And let us not forget that thousands of women suffered martyrdom for their unswerving devotion to Christ. To list them all would be impossible. As examples I would mention *Blandina, Perpetua,* and *Felicitas,* all of whom suffered persecution and cruel executions, in the late second and early third centuries, for refusing to pay homage to Caesar.[30]

I learned much about early church history when I lived in Italy and visited the catacombs. In the early church, women appeared in every reference to ecclesiastical orders. The term *presbyteress* designated an Apostolic order. The term *widow,* like *elder,* was a title of seniority and was never used in Roman epigraphy to denote a woman who had lost her husband. In catacomb frescoes, women bishops and elders are pictured seated in Episcopal chairs. In two inscriptions dating from the reign of Pope Pascal I, the word *episcopa,* (bishop) appears on the catacomb tombs of women. It was evidently the will of the Divine Emancipator that women also be ordained to the Christian ministry.

WOMAN'S EMANCIPATION

On the day of Pentecost the Holy Spirit, the Divine Emancipator, set women free — free from bondage to the law and to tradition. "For each one of you" — women as well as men — "is no longer a slave, but a son" — or daughter — "and an heir"[31] — free from the fear of man and of public opinion, free from every kind of fear!

The person going into the ministry should receive all that scholarship can give. But, most of all, he or she needs that which Jesus told his disciples to wait for — namely, *the enduement of power from on high.*[32]

"For God hath not given us the spirit of fear; but of power, and of *love,* and of a *sound mind.*"[33] These gifts, granted by enduement from the Holy Spirit, are the primary needs of those who are called to preach the word of God and minister to his people.

Chapter Four

WHAT DID PAUL REALLY SAY?

Throughout the major part of Christian history, those who opposed women's preaching and ministry have quoted the writings of the Apostle Paul to justify their opposition. Particularly is this true of the words in his first letter to the Corinthian Church, which read, "Let your women keep silence in the churches, for it is not permitted unto them to speak."[1] In the Jerusalem Bible we read, "Women are to remain quiet at meetings. They must remain in the background as the Law lays down."

DID PAUL FORBID WOMEN TO PREACH?

If Paul intended for this passage to be understood as prohibiting women to prophesy or preach, he was contradicting one of his earlier statements. He had already written instructions as to how a woman should be attired when she prayed in public or prophesied. "Every woman that . . . *prophesieth* with her head uncovered dishonoreth her head."[2]

"Every woman that . . . prophesieth!" How could a woman prophesy, or preach, while, at the same time, keeping silent?

(Incidentally, we no longer think it is forbidden for a woman's head to be uncovered in church, nor is it thought of as a disgrace, as Paul wrote, for men to have long hair. Paul and translators speak plainly of these instructions as having been "traditions, rules, and customs" in the churches in those days. They have nothing whatever to do with preaching.)

In the New Testament, the terms *prophesy* and the *gift of prophecy* are used by translators to convey such meanings as: *Speaking God's message*[3]; *Speaking words that build up, encourage, and console*[4]; *Inspired preaching*[5]; the *gift of preaching the word of God.*[6]

Nowhere in his writings did Paul forbid women to prophesy or preach. This he would not have dared or even wanted to do, thus interfering with the prerogatives of the Holy Spirit

There must, therefore, be a misunderstanding of that "silence" passage.

In Paul's time it was customary for men and women to be segregated in Christian meetings. Sometimes the apostle's preaching or teaching might be too profound for the uneducated minds of the women, and they might become noisy, interrupting the speaker with too many questions or voicing objections. Or perhaps they might talk among themselves.

The prohibition to women is explained in the context, "If they have questions . . . let them ask their husbands at home."[7] (I feel sorry for the women who had no husbands!) A woman who is prophesying (preaching) is not seeking to learn; on the contrary, she is involved in imparting knowledge.

On one occasion in Chicago I was asked to address the women officers of the Salvation Army. The men officers asked permission to attend. I said they might do so if they sat in the gallery. During my address I referred to this passage of Scripture and said: "One who preaches does not want to be interrupted with questions, and if the men in the gallery desire to learn or ask questions, let them ask their wives at home." The audience exploded with laughter.

The best explanation of this "silence" passage was given by Katharine Bushnell in her scholarly book, *God's Word to Woman,* privately published in 1926 and widely

read in England and America. She devoted years to research in the British Museum and was the first woman to
translate the Scriptures. In dealing with this passage she
asserted that Paul was answering a letter which had been
written to him, basing her assertion on Paul's words:
"What? came the word of God out of you? or came it
unto you only?" I found confirmation for this in Helen
Barrett Montgomery's careful, easily readable translation
of the New Testament:

> In your congregation (*you write*), as in all the
> churches of the saints, let the women keep silence in
> the churches, for they are not permitted to speak.
> On the contrary let them be subordinate, as also
> says the law. And if they want to learn anything, let
> them ask their own husbands at home, for it is
> shameful for a woman to speak in church. What, was
> it from you that the word of God went forth, or to
> you only did it come? [8]

A thirty-page thesis, explaining that Paul's words
had been misinterpreted, was written by the first woman
ever ordained to the ministry in the United States. In 1848,
while she was a student at the Oberlin Theological Seminary (she was ordained in 1853 by the Congregational
Church), Antoinette Brown pointed out that the Greek
word which had been translated as to *speak* meant literally
to *chatter* — to make the "sound of monkeys." She con-
cluded from this that Paul was merely cautioning women
to "speak wisely and not to babble." Her professor was so
impressed that he had her paper published in the Oberlin
Quarterly. [9]

The pages that have been written by scholars
attempting to interpret this short Scriptural passage could
fill a small library. All to correct a simple mistake made by
an early translator. I repeat that nowhere in his writings
did Paul forbid a woman to prophesy or "speak God's
message."

TRADITION AND THE
CHRISTIAN STANDARD

If we try to reconcile each individual statement in Paul's letters with his *actions,* we discover seeming inconsistencies. He wrote, for example: "Personally, I don't allow women to teach, nor do I ever put them in positions of authority over men ... (My reasons are that man was created before woman)."[10] But Paul did not always act in accordance with this statement.

To understand such apparent discrepancies we must take into account the customs, standards, and laws of the period in which early Christians lived.

It was Paul, let us remember, who raised for the church of all time the magnificent Christian standard: "There is neither Jew nor Greek, there is neither bond nor free, there is neither male nor female: for ye are all one in Christ Jesus."[11] All are ONE. No distinction of race. No class or social distinction. No sex distinction.

(Yet slavery was not abolished for centuries. And, to our shame, race, class, sex prejudice and discrimination continue to this day — saddest of all, in the churches.)

This Christian ideal, stated so positively by Paul, was a threat to strongly entrenched Hebrew traditions which clearly defined the distinctions between Jew and Gentile, master and slave, man and woman. Paul's ideal advocated abolishing the Roman law of slavery and erasing the Hebrew and Roman restrictions concerning the subjugation of women

The early church could not completely disregard Greek, Roman, Hebrew, and Middle Eastern customs without risking disgrace and sacrificing the hope of gaining converts. Traditions, prejudices, and discriminations cannot be altered overnight. Attempting to abolish them too swiftly can lead to revolution. Resistance to new ideas must be handled with caution, and progress is often painstakingly slow.

(Perhaps the greatest illustration of this is the persistent attitude of discrimination towards Blacks which many white Christians reveal even today.)

Considering his times, Paul went remarkably far in implementing his great Christian principle of equality. Let us consider what this involved.

First: The Question of Jew and Gentile

From the time of his conversion on the road to Damascus, Paul sought to eliminate the Jewish law of Hebrew superiority over Gentiles. He declared that Gentiles had equal rights to the Gospel. He was opposed by the first church in Jerusalem, and even differed with Peter on the subject. But he won. He is rightly called "the apostle to the Gentiles."[12]

Second: The Question of Slavery

Paul returned the escaped slave, Onesimus, to Philemon, his master, thus respecting Roman law. He did not ask Philemon to set Onesimus free; but, in his letter to Philemon[13] which Onesimus carried, Paul requested that Onesimus be treated, not as a slave, but rather as a brother — *"as you would myself."* He also promised to repay any money Onesimus might have stolen, even though (and this makes me smile) he reminded Philemon that he owed his own soul to him — to Paul.

In the same letter, Paul pointed out that he could have *commanded* Philemon to carry out his wishes, but that he preferred to send a *request* instead, leaving Philemon free to act voluntarily. He even appealed on the basis of his old age.

Obviously it was a personal sacrifice, "like sending my very heart," for Paul to send Onesimus back to his master. While in prison he had won Onesimus to Christ — "begotten him in my bonds" — and the grateful slave had

given him loving care and devoted service "in your stead
... He has become useful to me and will be to you," he
told Philemon.

His letter made it impossible for Philemon to refuse
("I know that you will do even more than I ask"), which,
in any case, he would have been unlikely to do, since he
himself was also the spiritual child of Paul.

This letter, the shortest chapter in the Bible, is a
masterpiece of literature, revealing Paul's ability to utilize
psychological insights and techniques that did not become
generally recognized and accepted until centuries later. He
also demonstrated a sense of humor and of pathos.

It is quite probable that his fellow Christians gave
Onesimus the opportunity, at a meeting of the church in
Philemon's house, to testify to the new birth which he had
experienced through Paul's influence, example, and teaching while sharing his imprisonment. Such an event — a
slave addressing a congregation — would represent a great
victory for Paul's principles.

Third: The Question of Race and Color

As I stood where Paul had stood, on Mars Hill in
Athens, Greece, I recalled with awe the remarkable statement he addressed to the people of that great city: "God
has made *of one blood* all the peoples of the world."[14] He
knew by revelation what science could not prove until
centuries later.

"Of one blood."

Even today, when science gives evidence of the
truth of that statement, we forget it; and races — black,
white, yellow, red — discriminate against each other. *Of all
people, Christians of every race should take Paul's words
to heart, for not only are they one by blood, but also by
grace are they one in Christ.* Discrimination and snobbery
are ugliest when found in the church.

Fourth: The Question of Sex

Since Paul was raised as a rabbi in the School of Gamáliel, it was a miracle of grace for him to be freed to such an extent from bondage to the Hebrew laws and customs of his day — free enough to open his mind and heart to concepts about women which ran counter to so much that he had learned in the past.

It might be remembered that, in an ancient prayer, the Jew thanked God that he was born neither a slave nor a woman. (We do know, however, that Mosaic Law recognized the rights of woman and honored her more than any of the coexistent philosophies of the East.) In Paul's day, the subordination of women was taken for granted in Hebrew doctrine, and in Greek and Roman as well. Roman laws taught the "perpetual tutelage of women."[15] This idea was so basic to Paul's orientation that he saw no inconsistency in stating that Christ was the head of man and man the head of woman,[16] while at the same time declaring that all believers were equal members of the body of Christ (needing each other on an equal basis) of which *Christ was the head.*[17] Neither was he troubled by inconsistency when he wrote that the unmarried woman was free to please the Lord but that the wife must first please her husband,[18] even though he also claimed that in all things *Christ* should have preeminence.[19]

PAUL AND WOMEN TEACHERS

Concerning Paul's instructions to Timothy, forbidding women to teach or usurp authority over men,[20] it should be remembered that the young church came into being in the midst of an exceedingly corrupt society. Christians were accused of foul practices and also of giving women unheard-of privileges. In an effort to avoid as many difficulties as possible, both Peter and Paul urged "subjection to every law of man for the Lord's sake,"[21] and "giving no occasion for stumbling in anything, that ministry be not blamed."[22]

And yet, much as he wished to avoid controversy, Paul's respect for women and his knowledge of their potential kept emerging. This was particularly evident when he wrote his second letter to Titus ("my true son"), who was in charge of the church in Crete. He advised Titus to encourage older women to set high standards and to be a good advertisement for the Christian faith. They were to be good examples for younger women, helping them to learn how to join with their husbands in practicing Christian ideals of purity and charity.[23]

An outstanding example of the potential Paul recognized in women was *Thecla.* The epistle known as the *Acts of Paul and Thecla,* which I have already mentioned, was quoted as early as the second century to prove woman's right to baptize. In this document Thecla is called an *apostle.* "Here," wrote Dr. Lee Anna Starr, "was a woman holding highest office in the New Testament Church. Instead of administering reproof, the Apostle Paul sends her greetings."[24]

As for *Priscilla,* one of Paul's esteemed disciples, he addressed her affectionately as "Prisca" and called her his "fellow-worker." Yet scholars agree that she taught the Scriptures to Apollos, who was himself renowned for his intellect and for his teaching skill. Priscilla was, in fact, a "teacher of teachers,"[25] but Paul never protested her activities. (The same description, "teacher of teachers," was also given to Catherine Booth,[26] another woman who lived up to Paul's expectations. I wonder what he would have done with her!)

I once heard a prominent New York preacher remark that he could imagine Priscilla being asked, by her husband Aquila, to cook a nice dinner while *he* taught

Apollos the Scriptures — and then inviting Priscilla to join them in prayer! Ignorance and arrogance go hand in hand.

When addressing ministers I have often said: "Brothers, if you want to honor Paul's remark that women should not teach or exercise authority over men, you must dismiss all of the women who teach classes or hold administrative positions in your churches or in your missions, and, at the same time, open your pulpits to the inspired preaching of spirit-filled women."

The church has done the very opposite, thus affirming that sex bias and fear of competition, rather than any words of Paul's, have constituted the basis for discrimination against women as ministers.

Paul wrote that *the letter* (of the law) kills, but *the spirit* gives life,[27] and that all Christians, men *and* women, should stand fast *in the liberty* wherewith Christ has set them free, and not be entangled again in the yoke of bondage.[28]

Paul also declared that in the Lord "neither is woman independent of man, nor is man independent of woman; for just as the woman was made from the man, so also is the man born of the woman, while they both come from God."[29]

Let us keep in mind that *principles* are the same at all times and under all conditions; and that *principles* — not hard and fast rules and regulations — must be our guide to the mind of Christ and to his will for the time in which we live.

Chapter Five

THE GRADUAL REPUDIATION OF
WOMAN'S GOD-GIVEN LIBERTY

WOMEN IN THE MIDDLE AGES

For fifteen centuries, women of intellect and holiness functioned throughout Europe as ordained abbesses and queens, with the authority of bishops. Noblewomen who were also Christians often insisted on provisions in their marriage contracts guaranteeing them the right to practice their religion, and many converted their husbands to Christianity. The first Anglo-Saxon Christian church in England was established by a woman, Bertha, the granddaughter of King Clovis I of France. (His queen, Clotilda, had agreed to marry him only on the condition that she be permitted to remain a Christian. She had converted the king, and in the year 496 he became the first major barbarian leader to the baptized.)

Bertha's daughter, Ethelberga, married and converted Edwin, the King of Northumbria; and his great-niece, Hilda, was baptized with him in 627.

Dedicating her life to the service of God, Hilda served for twenty years (660 to 680) as Abbess of Whitby, one of the numerous "double-monasteries" in which men and women participated as equals, both in England and on the continent during the seventh and eighth centuries. All were administered by women. According to Nancy Hardesty,[1] these abbesses participated as equals with bishops, lords, and kings in councils of church and state. Their monasteries were "the universities of their day, the only places where intellectual and artistic pursuits were undertaken." They were also "centers for evangelistic outreach, spreading the Gospel among the surrounding pagans and instructing them in the faith."

But double-monasteries, along with the equal rights of women, were doomed to die in the Middle Ages. Ascetic ideals were gradually introduced, resulting in the adoption of celibacy by members of the clergy, and this revolutionized their attitudes toward women. Church fathers began to regard them as the embodiment of temptation (except those dedicated to virginity). Some of their writings contain unquotable passages vituperating woman — condemning her as the source of all evil. All the sins of the human race were charged against her. In some ancient paintings sin is represented as a serpent with a woman's head. [2]

The effects of this attitude of mind, though fast disappearing, are still evident in some parts of the world. As illustration, I was the only woman to be admitted to the palace of his excellency Archbishop Spiridon of Greece in 1951. The purpose of my visit was to discuss with him the desirable union of all Christians of the world. The archbishop enthusiastically endorsed my views. As I mounted the marble steps of the palace, dressed in my preaching robe, I became aware of the piercing gaze of the young monks standing on either side and at the top of the stairs. They looked at me as though I were a strange creature from another world.

My interpreter for this meeting and for the sermons I delivered was Father Jerome Kotsonis, the assistant to the archbishop, who has now succeeded him. As I was departing, Father Kotsonis said to me, "Your ministry has been a personal blessing to me"; and even today he still takes an interest in my activities. [3]

Mrs. Demarest with Archbishop Spiridon of the Greek Orthodox Church, Athens, Greece, and Father Jerome Kotsonis, Secretary to the Archbishop and interpreter for Mrs. Demarest's preaching.

THE COUNCIL OF TRENT

The Council of Trent, which lasted for nineteen years (1545 to 1564), had among its results the total appropriation of all ecclesiastical authority by the male clergy. This male monopoly of the clergy continued throughout the Reformation and its resultant Protestant churches. This was the logical continuation of a process that had been going on for centuries as, systematically, step by step, women were stripped of the freedom and equality which the Holy Spirit had granted them at Pentecost.

Fortunately these developments in no way minimized the effect on all Christendom of the great women of the Roman Church — such saints as Catherine of Sienna, Theresa of Spain, Catherine of Genoa — and others to the present date, such as Mother Cabrini (St. Francis Xavier Cabrini) of Lombardy, Italy, whom thousands of American children and nuns consider to be their spiritual mother. *The operations of the Holy Spirit have never been confined to or limited by the organized church.* There have always been courageous women, in or out of the church, who preached and ministered in obedience to him.

THE WALDENSIANS

Among the first were the Waldensian women of northern Italy. They were members of free fraternal associations (the earliest Protestants) which were founded between 1170 and 1180 by Peter Waldo, a wealthy, middle-class merchant of Lyon. Somehow Waldo secured a Bible and had sections of it translated into popular language. He distributed his goods among the poor and dedicated himself to preaching throughout Northern Italy calling on the people to repent and follow the Gospel.

The men and women who were members of his groups considered themselves to be "apostles of Jesus." They upheld the right of all believers, laity or clergy, whatever their sex, to preach. They rejected swearing, violence, and falsehood. They denounced the compromises established through the centuries between the Christian community and the political leaders, compromises which were begun in the age of Constantine.

In succeeding centuries Waldensians were massacred by the thousands — victims of the prejudices of church and state. Whole villages were burned. The great massacre of 1655, called the "Piemontese Easter," was immortalized by Milton's sonnet, "Avenge Oh Lord." But always some survived to bear aloft the torch of liberty and Gospel truth. Many times hounded across the border into Switzerland, they always came back to their beloved valleys.

Before the Reformation of the sixteenth century they were scattered; they hid in the mountains; they conducted their services in any place.

The Waldensian Church can truly be called the "Mater Reformationis" (the Mother of Reformation). Its suffering prepared the way for the Reformation.

Between the years 1532 and 1535 the Waldensians translated the complete Bible into French. They presented it to Reformation leaders as a token of union. The first Waldensian church was built in 1555. Today their work, spiritual, educational, social, is recognized and respected by the government of Italy — and, increasingly, by the Roman Church.

(In 1951, I preached in the Waldensian churches of Naples, Florence, Venice, and Rome, and visited their center in their northern valleys. My sermons were either in French or in English according to the language which the officiating minister could translate into Italian. At one time the eloquence of my interpreter was so great that I stopped preaching and told my audience he was a better preacher than I was! — which he had to translate, to the amusement of the audience. Their work, unique in a country where there was approximately one Bible for 100,000 people, commands respect. I love the Waldensians whom I found to be simple, humble, and truly dedicated people. Their ministers are highly intelligent and well educated.) [3]

THE REFORMATION

It is to be regretted that the Reformation, that great movement for the freedom of man's spirit, did not similarly recognize woman's rights, her spiritual freedom, and the scriptural basis for, and efficacy of, her ministry.

At the cost of immeasurable suffering, sacrifice, and the martyrdom of thousands throughout Europe, the Reformation broke the chains that bound the Bible to lecterns in monasteries and abbeys and gave it to the common man in his native language. This great movement emphasized the principle of "the priesthood of all believers." It enshrined the concept of the dignity of every individual soul, the right of private judgment, the freedom to discover and declare the mind of God, and went so far as to admit this could not be confined to one sex alone. And yet, ignoring the example set by Jesus, and overlooking Paul's many other actions and statements on the subject of women, it isolated one single line — "let your women keep silence" — from a fragment of a single letter, and declared it to be *the divine ruling of all time* regarding the position of women in the Church!

"One of the most brilliant proofs of St. Paul's genius," George Meredith once remarked, "was the discovery that women could be employed with effect in the service of the Church." If this were his discovery, the apostle would be much troubled if he could know how misinterpretations of his injunctions to the Corinthian Church have been used to cripple the female ministry ever since.[4]

Reformation leaders declared that the home was a sufficient sphere for women's ministry. Luther said she was to "remain at home, sit still, keep house, and bear and bring up children." Calvin and John Knox also forbade her any other calling. It remained for George Fox and his Quakers, and the Salvation Army, to uphold woman's spiritual equality and her right to preach the Gospel.

THE REWORDING OF THE SCRIPTURES

The Lord speaks. The enemy flees. The women at home cry out the happy news. . . .

So reads the eleventh verse of Psalm 68 in *The Living Bible Paraphrased,* published in 1971.

Such a statement hardly seems a threat to male ministry.

But, as Katherine Bushnell pointed out in *God's Word to Women,* which I have previously mentioned, the words "The women" were omitted from all translations except the original.

The translators of the King James version did not have access to the original. And so, in their words, the same verse reads as follows:

The Lord gave the word: great was the company of those that published it.

The Bible, woman's divine charter of liberty, was undoubtedly tampered with by translators, who transformed it into a tool that would force her into a yoke of bondage[5] subjecting her to the traditions of men.

Dr. Lee Anna Starr, in her book entitled *The Bible Status of Women,*[6] exposed the manner in which translators and church officials achieved this objective. According to Dr. Starr: The hierarchs of Christendom . . . men who sat in council . . . framed laws to degrade woman. Through their emissaries, the missionaries and delegated clerics, they imposed the [Roman] law of "Patria Potestas" in almost all its main features on the womanhood of Christendom for well nigh two thousand years. . . They permitted the expurgation of women's names from sacred manuscripts; the transposing and changing of the feminine into the masculine; the altering of entire sentences, as in the Codex Beza . . . Bishops and archbishops active in State affairs . . . gave voice and vote in favor of laws to oppress woman. ... Translators used "divers weights and measures" in rendition of God's word. ... Exegetes tortured Hebrew and Greek syntax to make it express their own thought. .. Expounders of Sacred Writ, in pulpit and on seminary rostrums, exchanged the truth of God for a lie. .. Commentators whose dissertations lade the shelves of ecclesiastical libraries implanted erroneous ideas as to woman's true place in Divine economy.

The women of the world, it would seem, may be justly grieved that church authorities sanctioned such misinterpretations, mistranslations, and misapplications of the Scriptures. Dr. Starr's research provides the evidence. All women, and men as well, who hunger and thirst for righteousness and justice will thank her for it. .. and be grateful as well for the courage and self-sacrifice of the many women in or out of the churches, who, through the centuries, have defied the intolerant, arrogant concept of male superiority.

TWO THOUSAND YEARS AFTER PENTECOST

As the twentieth century approached, attitudes from the middle ages still prevailed in many segments of the church. But dedicated women were expanding their activities and extending their humanitarian influence.

"The work which the female ministry has accomplished and is accomplishing," wrote W. T. Stead in 1900, "is work which men have hitherto, with all their monopoly, largely left undone." And, he added, "To forbid any willing worker because she does not happen to belong to our sex is one of those fantastic and horrible offenses against God and man which may justly be described as a mystery of iniquity and the abomination of the earth."[7]

W. T. Stead's comments were made in his biography

of Catherine Booth, about whom Dr. Starr declared:

> The Church of England afforded no room for the talent and energy of Catherine Booth, "The Mother of the Salvation Army," so she took her stand by the side of her husband, William Booth, in the work of evangelizing the degraded classes in London. She became a preacher and turned many to righteousness. She was the mother of eight children, seven of whom became preachers. One of these, Catherine Booth-Clibborn, has a family of five sons and five daughters, and eight of these are preachers. The Salvation Army was organized in 1861 and in the brief period that has elapsed since then has assumed world proportions. [This was published in 1926.] Humanly speaking, this would be impossible had the Salvation Army, like the church, failed to recognize the equality of the sexes.[8]

Yet Dr. Starr had to add the following comment about Catherine Booth's daughter-in-law (whose unique activities devoted to the reformation of the inmates of American prisons began in 1896):

> The church had no room for the ministries of Maud Ballington Booth, so she wended her way to jails and penitentiaries, with God's word in her hand, and His love in her heart, and today an army inside prison walls, and thousands who have served their term and been released revere her as "The Little Mother."[8]

(Little progress had been made since the days when the Reverend Samuel Wesley reprimanded his wife, who raised her sons John and Charles to become beacon lights in the church. Why was the Rev. Wesley angry at his wife? Because she gathered her servants and her neighbors together to read and discuss the Scriptures!)

One of the thousands of examples of prominent

American women of the past century whose God-given
liberty was repudiated by their church was Frances Willard[9]
— called "the greatest woman philanthropist of her generation" when, in 1905, her statue was placed in the rotunda
of the nation's Capitol as one of the most illustrious citizens of the State of Illinois. In 1910 she was similarly
enshrined in the Hall of Fame, located at New York University. As President of the Evanston College for Ladies,
she had been the first woman ever to hold such a title.
When this college merged with Northwestern University,
she became Dean of its Women's College. But she gave up
her career as educator because she was possessed by a compulsion to help "poor, battered humanity."

The greatest achievement of her life was the founding of the Woman's Christian Temperance Union which
became *the largest women's organization the world had
ever known.* Like my grandmother, my mother and myself,
she fought "to rescue the Living Christ in human hearts
from the enemies that defile the temple of God." Her conviction, upheld by the Supreme Court, was that the government was responsible to preserve and protect the people—
hence her efforts for prohibition.

It was she who originated the Social Creed of the
Churches, which was first issued by a single denomination
in 1908 (thirty years after she wrote it) and adopted a few
years later by the Federal Council of Churches (now the
National Council of Churches). James Strahan called her
"one of the saints of the modern calendar."

Miss Willard's biographer, Anna Adams Gordon,
described her in these lines:

> How Christlike she became the whole world
> knows. . . Rarely has the world seen so complete a
> death of self, so far as personal aims are concerned
> . . . to many a manly heart was revealed through her
> the truth that there is neither male nor female in
> Christ Jesus.

In her own journal Miss Willard wrote:

> When will the stronger member of the human family in every land discover that if he uses his more muscular arm to hold down to the earth the weaker member, he is putting the knife to his own breast — signing the death-warrant of his own manhood? That two and two make four is not more capable of demonstration than that in every age and country woman has been the stone around man's neck to sink him to the lowest depths or the winged angel to help him to the purest heights that he has ever won.

Frances Willard truly believed that God had called her to the ministry. However, as she poignantly said in her book, *Glimpses of Fifty Years*,[10] "Even my dear old mother-church, the Methodist, did not call women to her altars. I was too timid to go without a call. . . ." But she did urge younger women who felt a similar call, to be persistent in their efforts to enter the doors that had been closed to her. And she begged all Christian people who "grieve over the world's great heartache," to encourage every "true and capable woman, whose heart God has touched, in her wistful purpose of entering upon that blessed Gospel ministry."

On one occasion, during a temperance campaign in Pittsburgh, Miss Willard, who had been invited to sit on the platform, was requested, by the director, to offer a few words of prayer. As she was about to begin, a pastor arose and compelled her to stop. The meeting was being held in his church, the Methodist Protestant on Fifth Avenue, and he declared that no woman could offer audible prayer in a church where he was in charge. Miss Willard sat down and wept.

Frances Willard was only one of the hundreds of women who sought and found other outlets for their talents and their humanitarianism. Some of them founded, alone or as partners with their husbands, not only the Salvation Army but also such organizations as the Red Cross, the Young Women's Christian Association, and the Volunteers of America. "The brainy women members of our churches," one bishop complained, "are going more and more into club work, and more and more into politics, while they should be devoting themselves to the church."[11]

One young woman, Welthy Honsinger, had this to say about the bishop's complaint:

> I do know that when a young woman of our church leaves college halls today, she has an intelligent idea of every vocation, from aviation to brokerage, and may enter every one except the ministry. She may become a policeman or a judge, she may be a mayor or a senator, but she may not be ordained as a minister of the Gospel of Christ. So the young women of trained intellect and talent, as they come out to take their share in the world's work, specialize, in increasing numbers, in law, and not a few have become judges. They specialize in journalism and become editors; they specialize in education and become college presidents, but they may not, in the name of the Father, receive a child into the church nor administer the sacrament to the dying. [12]

As a student at Syracuse University, Welthy Honsinger had become a member of Pi Beta Phi, the first of the social-inspirational-philanthropic organizations established in the latter half of the nineteenth century by idealistic young Christian women who had found their way into the universities and were attempting to define and understand their responsibilities toward each other and toward the communities in which they lived. Miss Honsinger's studies prepared her for a career in grand opera. But in 1903, at the age of twenty-four and alone, she left her home in Rome, New York, to live in China, then France, and finally India. In 1905 she became headmistress of a mission school in Nanchung, China. In 1924 she married Frederick Bohn Fisher, Methodist Bishop of Calcutta and Burma. He died in 1938, and for the next eight years she traveled and lectured on international relations and became a close friend of Mahatma Gandhi, who urged her to work in the villages of India. From 1948 to 1952 she was Chairman of the United Church Women World Day of Prayer. In 1953, when she was seventy-four years old, she founded a school, *Literacy House*, at Allahabad, India. A new campus of this school, which she established in Lucknow, India, in 1956, is now known as *Literacy Village*. It has grown into a world-wide organization — *World Education, Incorporated* — which is financed by private contributions and the governments of India and the United States.[13] At the age of ninety, Mrs. Fisher was still functioning as its President. Many American universities have presented her with honorary degrees; and in India she received the first Nehru Literacy Award.

What the church has lost, by making the ministry unavailable to such women, can never be computed. Even sincere women church members are so unaccustomed to seeing and hearing women in the pulpit that many of them feel uncomfortable at the idea of women as ministers. They have been conditioned by their own society to disavow their own potential. They have no knowledge of the spiritual heights certain women are capable of achieving, if only given the chance.

The majority of these women, not to mention their male associates, are not even aware that the church was the first institution to recognize the equality of women. They do not realize that Christ and the Holy Spirit pointed the way. No one has explained to them that God is not bound by human limitations . . . that to him barriers of race, class, wealth, sex, do not exist . . . that he calls whom he wills and uses whom he wills, whether it be man or woman.

But a few women at the turn of the century were still struggling to keep this cause alive, and they were assisted by a few enlightened men who understood and offered reinforcement. Through the efforts of such individuals, through their devotion to righteousness and justice, the work of the Holy Spirit, as Divine Emancipator, will ultimately prevail.

The following lines by a famous contemporary poet beautifully illustrate one man's capacity to recognize injustice and to transcend prejudice and partisanship. May it help others to grow in understanding and compassion.

ROBBERS' DEN

They have taken Sun from Woman
And consoled her with Moon;
They have taken Moon from Woman
And consoled her with Seas;
They have taken Seas from Woman
And consoled her with Stars;
They have taken Stars from Woman
And consoled her with Trees;
They have taken Trees from Woman
And consoled her with Tilth;
They have taken Tilth from Woman
And consoled her with Hearth;
They have taken Hearth from Woman
And consoled her with Praise —

Goddess, the robbers' den that men inherit
They soon must quit, going their ways,
Restoring you your Sun, your Moon, your Seas,
Your Stars, your Trees, your Tilth, your Hearth —
But sparing you the indignity of Praise.

— Robert Graves

Chapter Six

THE NEED FOR FEMININE MINISTRY

Humanity is both masculine and feminine. Is it not reasonable to assume, therefore, that it needs both a masculine and a feminine ministry?

My lifelong experience in the service of humanity, during which I preached the Gospel and ministered in many countries to all sorts of people — men and women, rich and poor, educated and unlettered, religious and irreligious — convinced me that feminine ministers *are* needed. They are needed by women, by men, by children, by the church, and by the world.

WOMAN'S NEED

Many a girl has confided to me that she would rather die than discuss her problems and confess her sins to a man, be he curate, minister, or bishop. Yet statistics indicate that females outnumber males in our society. Should girls who cannot consult a man be denied the help, advice, and consolation that a feminine minister could provide?

For years, in connection with my evangelistic campaigns in the United States, Canada, and Newfoundland, I gave special lectures for women and girls only. Such subjects as *Love, Courtship, Marriage, Motherhood, the Raising of Children*, and *Lessons I Learned from the Mother of Jesus* were included. The number of women attending ranged from one hundred to five thousand. On one occasion, in Richmond, Virginia, women actually tore each other's clothes in the scramble to enter a 5000-seat auditorium. My husband had to call the police to restore order. On another occasion, in Toronto, Canada, I was requested to repeat my lecture on *Love and Marriage.* I agreed to do so on the condition that only girls between the ages of fourteen and twenty-five be admitted. Women from all of the churches spread the word, and, as a result, the sanctuary, seating two thousand, was completely filled with young girls.

To convey the effects of these lectures would be impossible. Women would come to me, money in hand, tearfully begging for printed copies. But I never had time to prepare them. Wives would say, "I never knew what marriage meant until I heard you . . . I went home and kissed my husband for the first time in years. We had a talk, and I don't think we'll get a divorce." Elderly women lamented, "If only someone had told me these things when I was young." Young girls would say, "You have told me more in one hour than my mother told me in my whole life." Or they would say, "Now I know which boy to marry." The need of girls and women for feminine ministry was abundantly demonstrated.

In Toronto, where through the years I conducted twelve evangelistic campaigns, a delegation of women called on me to discuss my lectures. "Why is it," one of them asked, "that other lectures on sex and love and marriage make no impression on our college girls, but after hearing you they are changed?" I prayed for her to realize, without my telling her, that the change was wrought by the Spirit of God.

These were lectures, not sermons; my sermons were delivered in the churches quite separately. Nevertheless, I always prayed that my listeners would feel the authority of the Holy Spirit behind my words, even though *I did not mention him.* I was thrilled, therefore, when a woman in

Lexington, Kentucky, exclaimed to me, "I never believed in the Holy Spirit until I heard your lecture today, Mrs. Demarest."

A Roman Catholic priest once said to me, "I want to thank you for your lecture on the Holy Mother. The entire womanhood of our town has been affected for good."

Confessions I heard after these lectures often made me long for a spiritual bath. But the changed lives and the happiness of the women delivered made the effort worthwhile.

Confession is a very great human and spiritual need. But, because of woman's reluctance to consult male ministers on the questions relating to sex which are so prevalent in our society, the psychiatrist has, in many instances, replaced the minister. This is unfortunate, since the help needed is far more spiritual in nature than intellectual or psychological. That is why Christian psychologists study the ministry, and many ministers study psychology.

A young, unmarried woman of my acquaintance fell in love with a married man. One day she told me that she could no longer resist the temptation to accompany him on a weekend trip. In the middle of the night I woke up under a compulsion to write to her. I spared no words. My letter could have burned the paper. But it was written in love — love for her soul. When she received it she sobbed for three hours. But she was completely delivered from an unwholesome passion that could have wrecked not only her own life but also a happy home. This young woman's need for a feminine minister was evident.

Yes, women and girls need feminine spiritual ministry. But not merely women!

MAN'S NEED

Many a troubled man, after hearing me preach, has expressed gratitude that I was a woman, because my words enabled him at last to understand his wife — or because, as a wife, I could tell him where he had failed as a husband. Also, men have said that I helped them as no male minister could — just because I was a mother, in the natural as well as in the spiritual sense.

Sometimes, at the request of high school principals, I gave talks for boys only. On one occasion, some girls were waiting outside the door for a boy who was the handsomest and the "wildest" in that particular high school. As he emerged they pounced on him. "What did she say?" they asked. "How did you like it?" His face grew very red and he clenched his fists as he replied: "Why didn't anyone ever tell me these things before?"

Frequently, through the years, I delivered a lecture for men only. The title: *There is a Man.* These were the words which the queen of Chaldean King Belshazzar uttered when, uninvited, she entered the banquet hall and found the king shaking with fear. In the midst of an orgy with a thousand of his attendants, he had been terrified by the sudden inexplicable appearance of a mysterious hand which wrote an undecipherable message on the wall.

"Oh King," said the queen with calm dignity, "do not be alarmed. . . . In your kingdom there is a man in whom lives the spirit of God Most Holy . . . he will be able to tell what this means."

She was speaking of Daniel.[1]

"There is a man! Good news, indeed," I told my audiences of men. "Nothing is more noble in all creation than a man who is truly a MAN."

"What does it mean to be a MAN?" I would continue. Here was a king who was a slave — a slave to his passions, his wealth, his idols. By contrast, here was a slave — Daniel — who was a king, though he did not even own his own body. He flung the king's bribe into his face. "Let thy gifts be to thyself, and give thy rewards to another." But, he added, "I will tell thee the meaning of this writing."

Daniel reminded Belshazzar of what had happened to his father, King Nebuchadnezzar, when he had "hardened his heart in pride." And then Daniel pointed out, "You have not humbled yourself even though *you knew all this.*" Therefore, this writing on the wall, *Mene, Mene, Tekel, Upharsin,* means, *You have been weighed in the balance and found wanting.* Your kingdom will be taken from you and given to another. And that very night the king was slain.

The queen had evidently been observing Daniel, and had been greatly impressed by the godliness of his character.

"You are being watched more than you know," I would tell my male audiences. "Your wives, your children, your business associates, your churches, your country need men of whom it can be said 'There is a man' — not a weakling, not a baby, not a brute, not a quitter, not someone who can be bought — but a MAN."

A woman can tell an audience of men what no man could tell them — and they will take it. The tearful gratitude of wives moved me deeply. They told me how my lectures had affected their husbands. "You have told him what all my married life I wanted to tell him but could not," they would say.

One of these lectures, in Johnson City, Tennessee, was attended by about two thousand men. When it ended, two hundred of them were on their knees at the altar, confessing, repenting, making their peace with God. Among them was an ex-Congressman, turned industrialist. From that time on his relationship with his associates and his employees was revolutionized. His conversion also resulted in the forming of the Layman's Evangelistic League, of which he was president. This league, numbering one hundred, was composed of pharmacists, lawyers, doctors, the principal of a high school, business executives, and others. These men devoted certain hours every week to winning souls, even going to neighboring towns. When I returned to Johnson City eight years later, the league was still functioning with success.

A lawyer who had attended the meetings came to see me. He broke down and sobbed like a child. When he had recovered his self-control he confided that the deaths of his wonderful wife and of the little daughter he adored were, he believed, God's judgment for his sin. (For many years he had secretly been living with a mistress.)

"Before you came to our city," he told me, "I wrote to the newspapers saying that it was a sin for a woman to preach. But now I think it would be a sin if you did *not* preach."

The churches of the city had united under my leadership and, aside from the lectures, I preached every night and sometimes twice a day. At the end of one of the later meetings, this same lawyer approached me, leading by the hand a beautiful woman — his mistress. Her face was radiant. She too had been converted. Their consciences had become sensitized, and they wanted my advice. Did I think it would be permissible for them to marry — or should they agree to give each other up and never meet again?

I asked them to give me a day to pray about it. The next night I told them that since they had met the conditions of repentance and faith, God had forgiven them. Nevertheless, I suggested that they remain apart for a year, during which they would devote themselves to some form of Christian service aside from their regular work. If, at the end of the year, they still desired to marry, I believed God would sanction their union. They agreed.

Years later I visited them in their beautiful home. They were a very happy couple.

Another man on his way to a Sunday morning appointment with a prostitute saw, in front of a church, an announcement that a woman was preaching. Curious, he entered the church where I was speaking on the text, "Sir, we would see Jesus,"[2] the request which some Greeks made to the disciple Philip. Among other illustrations, I submitted that if a small child is found playing with a razor, the wise father will not scold him, for fear he may cut himself. Instead, he might hold out a toy or an apple. The child will drop the razor to reach for whatever is offered. Or, if a child is playing in a puddle and getting mud all over himself, the father might take him by the hand and show him the ocean, whereupon the child would forget the puddle.

"When you see Jesus," I said, "you just naturally let go of those sins that are destroying you."

"When you had finished I was like a drunken man," this man told me when we met a few years later. "I staggered out into the street, saying to myself, 'I have seen Jesus! I have seen Jesus!' Then I remembered my appointment. The thought of it was now repugnant. But I decided to visit the woman anyway and give her my witness, in the hope that she too might be changed."

The outcome was that this man studied for the ministry and was ordained a Presbyterian minister. He attended a certain summer conference of the Presbyterian denomination in which I was permitted to speak to a small group of women. I could not be one of the main speakers because I was a woman. In protest he told his story and said, "It is because of Mrs. Demarest that I am a minister." That man might never have heard the Gospel had not his curiosity to hear a woman preach led him into the church.

Another man who did not believe a woman should preach finally yielded to the heckling of his wife and daughter and came to hear me. Purposely he sat far in the back of the top gallery of the church. Afterwards he told me, "You had not been preaching for five minutes before I forgot whether you were man or woman. I heard the voice of God."

In a certain town at the end of a meeting, when I appealed for penitents to come to Christ, a man threw himself to his knees beside the platform and grasped my feet. "Please forgive me," he sobbed. "I have hated you and spoken all manner of evil against you; I have done all in my power to injure you. I must ask your forgiveness before I can ask God's." "You were forgiven before you asked," I assured him. "Now the important thing is for you to seek and receive divine forgiveness and a new heart."

One of my most humbling experiences was when a Doctor of Divinity, the minister of a church where I was preaching, came to me on the platform after I had delivered a sermon, "The Temple," which had been given to me in a dream. He took my hand in both of his and, with tears in his eyes, implored, "Let me be Silas to your Paul." Of course I did not feel worthy of that minister's words. I quote them only to show that he recognized in my preaching an apostolic ministry.

A profligate Texas millionaire and his mistress were converted in that meeting.

CHILDREN'S NEED

In 1918, when I married Agnew Demarest, the organist and choir master of the Second Presbyterian Church in Louisville, Kentucky, he was a widower, six years my senior. He had two little boys, ten-year-old John and eight-year-old Cornelius, so I didn't have to wait to be a mother! I loved those two boys as though I had borne them. Although later I bore six children of my own, the terms "stepmother" and "stepbrother" were never used in our home.

The boys' mother had died shortly after Cornelius was born, so they had never known a mother. One day, as John and I were sitting on the couch, Cornelius came to us on all fours and asked, "John, who do you love best, our first mother or our second mother?" John threw his arms around me and said: "You, you, you."

I was taken aback because I had earnestly sought to encourage the boys to think of and love their real mother, even though they had not known her. ("Do unto others as you would have them do unto you"; if I were replaced as a wife, I wouldn't want my children to forget me.) I said, "Oh no, John, you mustn't say that." He drew back, his face flushed, and said, "You don't understand."

Realizing that I had hurt his feelings I said gently, "Tell me, dear, why did you say that?" "Because you are our *spiritual* mother," he answered, "which other mothers are not." A revealing statement from a boy ten years old.

Through the years I have quoted his words to thousands of women attending my lectures. I have told them that any cat can have kittens, and that having a baby does not make a mother. A child needs more from a mother than just physical or mental care. A child needs spiritual care.

Like God, we are a trinity. He is Father, Son, and Holy Spirit. We are spirit, soul, and body. The spirit in man is the God-consciousness. The soul is the world-consciousness, the other-consciousness. The body is the self-consciousness. Since the spiritual life affects the soul-life and the physical-life, *it is the more important part of the human trinity and needs the most care.*

Today we are witnessing the appalling results of the neglect of the spiritual life of children.

I believe with all my heart in the conversion of children. I myself was converted when only six years old. Through the years I have held meetings for children from seven to fourteen years of age. On one occasion, in Newfoundland, there were over fifteen hundred children in the audience.

Some painful experiences have taught me to have no adult present in my children's meetings — no parent, no minister, no Sunday school teacher, though I would permit them to listen unseen. People often asked how I managed to hold the close attention of so many children for as long as an hour. It was easy. Children love stories. I illustrated the Gospel, and what it means to be a Christian, by telling them about a little street urchin in London, the son of a widowed, alcoholic father. I told them how this boy's conversion gave him new love and respect for his father and caused the father to be converted too.

If any little boy or girl started whispering and distracting the other children, I would stop speaking. The sudden silence would draw their attention back to me. I would quietly say, "You cannot listen to me and also to those children. When they stop whispering, I will continue." You may be assured there were no further disturbances.

I emphasized the importance of sincerity. To make sure that no child came to the altar just because he saw others coming, I had them close their eyes and come one by one. It was touching to see them come, holding their hands over their eyes. How often I would think that if only adults became as little children, as Jesus said, it would be easy for them to enter the kingdom of heaven.

I told the children that the word "conversion"

meant "turning" — turning *from* evil, which meant repentance, and turning *to* Christ, which meant faith. I told them
that if their conversion was genuine they could confess to
those against whom they had sinned, however painful it
was — and to their parents first.

I have heard every sin in embryo confessed to me by
children at the altar — even murder. The saddest experience was to hear children say so often, "You won't tell my
mother or my father will you?" By contrast, the prayers
of the children kneeling at the altar were beautiful to hear.

The results of these conversions would fill a book.
One boy, whose father had threatened to whip him if he
attended the meeting, went to his father and said he was
willing to take the whipping. And the father, instead of
carrying out his threat, came to a meeting himself and was
converted. During another meeting I saw a woman kneeling and weeping in a corner. When I knelt beside her and
asked her why she wept, she replied, "I want what my
little girl has."

As I was leaving one of the meetings after the children had scattered, a boy ran up with his cap in his hand.
"Is it too late?" he panted. "Too late for what, dear?"
"Too late to be converted." "It is never too late," I
answered. "You said, didn't you," he asked, "that if we
were sincere we would prove it by confessing and setting
things right? Didn't you say that?" "I certainly did." "Well,
I ran all the way home and got the gold watch I had stolen
and hidden under my mattress, and I gave it back to the
owner and told him I had no time to explain because I was
in a hurry to be converted." I said, "You *are* converted,
dear."

Years later I heard that some of these children had
gone into Christian service. Statistics have shown that the
most active church workers today were converted when
they were children.

Ministers and Sunday school teachers, whether men or women, should discuss together how best they can influence the lives of children. Every Sunday school should set a Day of Decision, and the children should be carefully prepared for that day. What is the use of telling Bible stories to children if not to inspire them to lead righteous lives? The sad fact is that many Sunday school teachers have themselves never been truly converted. How can a teacher teach a child to need a change of heart if his or her own heart has never been changed?

At age twenty-seven, Catherine Booth wrote:

> *What is conversion but a process by which those who are wrong are put right? As for the method by which this takes place, or the length of time it occupies, I have always been puzzled to understand why persons who believe in conversion at all should object either to the employment of any reasonable means, or to the speed with which they operate.*[3]

It is not necessary to know the day or the hour of one's conversion. Some experience a sudden dramatic change, while with others it may seem a slow realization of the grace of God. One thing is sure — a real Christian *knows* he is a Christian, for he has the witness of the Holy Spirit in his heart.[4] Some children seem to be filled with the Spirit from their mother's womb.

Many have asked me how early in life a child can be converted. I reply, "As soon as a child can differentiate between right and wrong." A three-year-old said to his mother, when she was tucking him into bed after she had brought him to one of my meetings, "The devil is stronger than I am, but Jesus is stronger than the devil." When the mother told me this, her eyes shining, she added, "If my child has truly learned this, it is worth all the meetings to me."

To my readers this reasoning may sound primitive—
even pitifully simplistic. Modern man has long since
abandoned the idea of a personal devil or a personal God.
He has explained away sin. Therefore, he needs no Savior.

The psychiatric couch or "workshop" has taken the
place of the altar of penitence. Science has pushed God
out of his heavens. Man has become his own God. Permissiveness has become the rule in the raising of children.

Now man is eating the bitter fruit of those trees.
Auswitz, the spread of nuclear bombs, the breakdown of
marriage and the home, the sex and drug madness of youth,
Watergate — all have created a deep sense of disillusionment, which, like a polluted fog, is obscuring man's reason
and vision. Exalted and yet diminished by his journey to
the moon, the realization of his littleness in the universe
has damaged man's pride and challenged his spiritual independence.

Let us hope that man, threatened economically and
militarily, threatened by world famine, may at last become aware of his inability, on his own, to save himself
or the little planet which is his home. The words of Jesus
have new force: What *does* it profit a man to gain the
whole world and lose his soul?[5] Man has sought to gain the
whole world and in the process has lost his soul.

Perhaps, after all, man will be happy to return, like
a child, to the altar of penitence, seek divine forgiveness,
and entreat the guidance which was so freely given to the
fathers of this country when they framed its Constitution.

THE CHURCH'S NEED

An Episcopal priest once said to me, "I wish you
could speak to our clergy throughout the land. You could
tell them what they never learn in theological schools."

Through the years I have had the privilege of addressing many meetings of ministers. I particularly remember one such meeting when the room was so full of smoke I could hardly breathe. But when I had finished we sank to our knees and the Holy Spirit hovered over us.

Throughout its history the church has needed and been benefitted by woman's ministry. Not only such men as John Huss (the Roman Catholic priest who declared, in 1401, that Christ, not Peter, was the foundation of the church and was burned at the stake for attempting to reform the church from within) . . . not only Martin Luther, John Calvin and Phillip Melanchthon (who one hundred years later brought the Reformation to its apex) . . . but also *women,* through those centuries, suffered, sacrificed, and were often martyred for their loyalty to their apostolic calling and their allegiance to the authority of the Scriptures.

In particular, I would mention two French women — one a Huguenot peasant girl, Marie Durand, and the other a Roman Catholic member of the nobility, Madame de la Mothe Guyon.

After the Edict of Nantes of Henry IV (1598), giving religious and political liberty to the Protestants of France, was revoked by Louis XIV in 1685, the Protestants were deprived of their religious and political rights and were severely persecuted, massacred, thrown into indescribably repulsive prisons — women as well as men. One of these women, *Marie Durand,*[6] was called "the soul of the resistance."

Because of the activities of her brother, Etienne Durand, a pastor who was martyred, she was separated from her fiance as a girl of sixteen and imprisoned with other Protestant women in *La Tour de Constance* at Aigues-Mortes. Although she was the youngest of the prisoners, she soon became recognized as their leader. As their spokesman, she corresponded with their families and friends, with authorities, and with the famous pastor, Paul Rabaut, who worked constantly to ease the plight of Protestant victims. She distributed whatever contributions came their way. She sang and preached, cajoled, encouraged and sustained them as the years lengthened into decades. Most of all, she inspired them to resist the temptation to recant, to succumb to the arguments and inducements of the Jesuit priests.

When I visited that somber jail, much like a tomb, where these valiant women had languished, I was shown the word "Resistez" (resist) which Marie had etched into the stone wall with a knitting needle. This one word she hoped would sustain the other women were she to be taken from them.

The most acute temptation to assail the women occurred once a month when they were allowed to breathe the fresh air of freedom on the roof of the prison. A heart-rending painting by Max Leehardt hangs in the *Musee de Montpellier*. It depicts these women leaning on the parapet, in various attitudes of grief and despair, as they gaze longingly at the green fields and forests of Languedoc and at the blue Mediterranean beyond. Knowing how cruelly the women were being tempted to utter the few words of recantation which would allow them to return to their homes, Marie Durand is not looking out at the country. She is pictured as standing in the middle of the roof, her head held high, singing!

In 1769, after almost half a century of imprisonment, Marie Durand's prayer was answered. She heard the words, *Vous etes libres* (You are free) uttered, in a voice filled with emotion, by Prince Charles de Beauveau, the new Military Governor of the Province of Languedoc. On his first visit to the cell in which fifteen women still existed he was so horrified by their plight that he arranged for their release.

A hymn of praise, led by Marie Durand, burst from the throats of the women. And when a soldier threw his cloak around Mlle. Durand, whose tattered clothes were falling from her body, she raised her arms heavenward and exclaimed, "Benissez, benissez la Seigneur." (Praise ye, praise ye, the Lord.)

As to Madame Guyon, although a Roman Catholic to the end of her life, *Jeanne Marie Bouvières de la Mothe Guyon*[7] (1684-1717) was also persecuted for her efforts to meet the spiritual needs of her church. Married at the age of fifteen, to a man many years her senior, she experienced years of almost continual persecution at the hands of her husband and her mother-in-law. These sufferings only reinforced her submission to the Lord and her determination that he alone should direct her. Before she was thirty-two her dying husband asked her forgiveness, declaring, "I did not deserve you." And her mother-in-law had become her devoted friend and supporter.

Turning down offers of marriage, the widowed Madame de la Mothe Guyon approached the Bishop of Paris and told him of her desire "to erect an establishment for all such as should be willing to give themselves to God without reserve." She was invited to participate in an establishment being launched by a group of New Catholics in Gex near Geneva.

"I felt myself to be invested with the apostolic state," she wrote. "From six in the morning until eight in the evening I was taken up in speaking of the Lord." As her renown as a spiritual guide increased, people flocked to her for counsel . . . friars, priests, and men of the world as well as simple peasants. "The Lord supplied me with what was satisfactory to them all," she said.

Her ministry gained her enemies as well as converts. Some church authorities supported her, others deliberately persecuted her. Bishop Jacques Benigne Bossuet was her principal enemy, whereas the famous Archbishop Francois Fenelon was her staunch friend and supporter. She never protested or complained. "Our Lord had destroyed in me every sort of natural antipathy," she commented.

Her inspired writings, eight books based on the Scriptures, astonished all who read them. Transcribers could not copy in five days what she wrote in a single night at the dictation of the Holy Spirit. Yet church authorities had her books on prayer burned in the market-place and continually threatened her. She was told that "it was only for churchmen to pray."

Her life, as described in an autobiography she was forced to write, was an agony of illnesses, betrayals, and persecution. Years were spent writing letters, books and beautiful poems in such deplorable prisons as Vincennes and the Bastille.

"Madame Guyon," said W. R. Inge in his introduction to her biography, "understood what Christianity means much better than her persecutors."

To offer another illustration of a woman's capacity to be of service to the church, I shall skip from the 18th century to a 19th-century incident in which my mother ministered to a Catholic priest. Dr. James Strahan recounted the story in *The Maréchale.*

On a lovely September evening (in Cannes, south of France) she was walking towards the sea, lost in admiration of the sunset. She observed a priest slowly proceeding towards the hill on which stood a little Catholic church. His appearance struck her; he looked at once so distinguished and so sad. An inner voice said to her, "Speak to that priest." Hurrying towards him, she said, "Good-evening, Mon Pére. I presume you are going to the church on the hill. May I accompany you, for I would speak with you on spiritual subjects?"

Uncovering his head, and bowing with great respect, he answered, "Certainly madame."

They walked on for a little in silence. Then she said, "What must I do to be saved, my Father?"

"Keep the ten commandments," he answered at once.

"But the rich young man who came to Jesus could say with his hand on his heart that he had kept them all, and yet had no assurance of salvation. He was in great trouble. He said 'What must I do to be saved?' "

"Oh, then you must take the holy Eucharist very often."

"But those who take it, my Father, are they saved from sinning? Are they not the victims of the power of evil, the same as others?"

"Oh! yes, Madame, but then there is the Confessional."

"But does not the same thing apply to the Confessional, my Father? You must know that there are tens of thousands in France who confess, but fall again the next day. They have not found rest. Is not Christ ready to save us if we are ready to be saved?"

"Alas! Madame, we shall sin always, always, to the very end of our lives."

"But, my Father, were not St. Augustine, St. Francis of Assisi, St. Catherine of Sienna, Fenelon and many others, delivered from the slavery of sin and self? They attained to something definite — to holiness." He turned with vehemence and said, raising his voice —

"Ah! Madame, but those were extraordinary lives. Those people were saints."

"No, my Father, they were men and women like you and me. What God did for St. Augustine or St. Catherine of Sienna, can He not do it for me if I am ready to fulfill the conditions which He lays down? What does religion do, what is it worth, if it cannot deliver us from sin?" He did not answer. He was silently thinking. She went on, "Is Christ a Saviour, yes or no?"

Catherine Booth-Clibborn
1858-1954
"The Marechale"

—Photo by Lizzie Caswell Smith

"Oh, yes, yes, yes, He is!"

"Has He saved *you*, my Father?" They stood still for a moment, and he turned his face away, with a look of poignant sadness. Then followed a confession — one of the deepest, most heartfelt cries she had ever listened to — ending with the words, "Alas, alas! all the days of my life I sin, and I expect to sin to my latest breath." The Maréchale was profoundly moved, and felt that she stood upon holy ground. At last she spoke —

"Then Calvary is the greatest fiasco the world has ever seen." Stretching out his hand, he said, "Oh Madame, do not say that; it is blasphemy."

"But, my Father, we are in the presence of facts, not fancies. You have left what men prize most. You have lived up to your light. And what do I find? Torment instead of rest, conflict instead of assurance, bondage instead of deliverance. Surely, my Father, Jesus did not come to increase our burdens, but to relieve them. You remember His word, 'Come unto me and I will give you rest.' He said, 'My yoke is easy and my burden is light.' Are these theories to be preached in pulpits, or are they realities?"

"My Father, how can you show others the way of deliverance if you have not found it yourself? How can you unbind if you are not unbound? How can you heal if you are not healed? How, my Father? Do you not see that all this is only from the head, not from the life, the heart?"

"It is true! But I try, oh, my God, I try!"

"But it does not come in that way — by our struggles."

"Then how?" he exclaimed in a tone of despair.

"Does He not say, 'Abide in me, and ask what you will, and it shall be done unto you'? Does not St. Paul testify, 'I can do all things through Christ which strengtheneth me'? How many have given praise to Him who is 'able to save to the uttermost' and 'able to present us faultless!' Put Him to the proof. If any one has the right to salvation, surely you have." They paused under a tree in the stillness of evening, and, while he stood with bowed head, she knelt beside him and prayed.

Just as there are spiritual fathers, so are there spiritual mothers. Human beings need both. Paul used the language of both when he said, "I have begotten you through the Gospel," and also, "I travail in birth."[8]

To "travail in birth" for souls and have the joy of seeing them born anew is an experience which should not be denied to any woman who knows herself called to the ministry. The birth of a soul is so vivid, so thrilling, so real and glorious and joyous that it can never be forgotten, whether experienced in oneself or witnessed in another. To be a mother, physically, is a glorious experience. To be a mother, spiritually, is even more wonderful.

The efficacy to the church of the spiritual ministry of women has been well demonstrated by those women who have been given the opportunity to do so. Let me describe an outstanding example. In Scotland, in 1951, I was guest preacher in a United Free Church, whose minister was a woman, the Reverend Elizabeth Barr. After the service, the session, composed entirely of men, waited on me to tell me, "Miss Barr is the best pastor, preacher, and administrator ever to have served this church. We cannot say enough in praise of her work. In our community she continually ministers in homes of destitution and even of crime. We are proud to be members of her session."

Elizabeth Barr was single. But there are many married women whose husbands and children have taken pride in their ministries, and have benefited as well. One of them baptized her own baby. Another performed the marriage ceremony for her son. I knew a husband and wife who were both ordained ministers, each serving a separate church. They would exchange notes and experiences. They would mutually assist each other and pray together for their churches and for their children, and these became outstanding Christian men and women.

It has been argued that a woman's ministerial career would prevent her from being a good wife and mother. That is not so. Her obligations and duties as wife and mother, rather than hindering, make her a better minister. It is often easier for her, as a "peer" to enter into and understand the lives of other wives and mothers and to advise and help them. As for her family, all of its members benefit from her broadened service and understanding. If we think of the church as a family, we can see how much it too can gain from the ministry of women who are also wives and mothers.

"The woman who would serve her generation according to the will of God," wrote Catherine Booth at age 26, "must make moral and intellectual culture the chief business of life. Doing this she will rise to the true dignity of her nature, and *find herself possessed of a wondrous capacity for turning the duties, joys, and sorrows of domestic life to the highest advantage, both to herself and to all those within the sphere of her influence.*"[9]

Conversely, being a minister can contribute insights that make a woman a good wife and mother.

Even if every other career were incompatible with wifehood and motherhood, the sacred office certainly is not. Women ministers, even more strongly than their secular sisters, believe in the sacredness of marriage and motherhood and are eager to set worthy examples. Natural motherhood contributes to spiritual motherhood and spiritual motherhood contributes to natural motherhood. Especially do working wives and mothers need the help, advice, and comfort that women ministers can give them.

Undoubtedly, combining the careers of wifehood, motherhood, and ministry, and seeking to do justice to all three, is not easy. It should only be undertaken by well-prepared, courageous, and highly dedicated women. Sometimes real suffering occurs, and much sacrifice is required. But suffering and sacrifice are what Christianity is made of. When accepted in the spirit of love, they bring forth rich fruit — and joy surpassing all other joys.

As a final example of women whose ministry met the church's need, I should like to say a few words about *Maude Royden*.[10]

The daughter of Sir Thomas Royden, chairman of the Cunard Steamship line, Maude Royden "was born for the pulpit and the spiritual life, and she was not the kind of person to be denied her vocation by the obstinate traditions of the past." So wrote A. C. Gardner in 1926.

Born into the Anglican church, which would not accept women as ministers, Miss Royden commented, "Women have prophesied, evangelized, converted from Priscilla to St. Catherine, of Siena, and from St. Catherine to Mrs. General Booth. It avails not. The church still says, 'Let the women keep silence.' Or . . . 'let them talk to one another [but] don't call it preaching and don't let it be in a church.' But the spirit of God, like the wind, blows where it lists, and even the English Church Union cannot prevent the inspiration descending upon a woman."

In 1918 an Anglican rector invited her to preach at a Good Friday service, but the Bishop of London intervened. After a brief but successful engagement as assistant minister at the City Temple, followed by several attempts to continue her work within the Anglican church, Miss Royden became the pastor of the Congregational church in Eccleston Square.

As the first woman to occupy Calvin's pulpit, Miss Royden preached in Geneva, where it was said of her, "Elle a la voix cathedrale."

With her resonant, musical voice and her unmistakeable sincerity and intelligence, Miss Royden championed the cause of equality for women in the pulpit and liberty for women — not as women but as citizens.

"Her piety is charged with a modern spirit and a freedom from cant that are always refreshing," declared Mr. Gardner.

Jane Addams called her "the greatest and wisest woman in England."

THE WORLD'S NEED

Church history records an unbroken line of women prophets. Though often unrecognized, opposed, and at times persecuted by both the traditional and established churches, they have spoken the word of God. Although held in contempt because of their sex, they have fought on joyously and victoriously, inspired by their unquenchable love for their Lord and Master. Some have blazed the trails for great revivals. Some have built churches where there were no churches and, when permitted, have ably pastored them.

On the mission field these women, even though unordained, have often been compelled by the Holy Spirit and by human need to fulfill the functions of the ministry or the priesthood. In the absence of recognized ministers or priests they have performed baptisms and marriages, offered Communion, pronounced the last rites, and conducted burial ceremonies.

I should like to mention two women in particular whose ministry met the world's need. Both of them also fulfilled admirably the roles of wives and mothers of large families. I am speaking of *Susannah Wesley* and *Catherine Booth*. The first mothered the Methodist Church. The second mothered the Salvation Army.

Susannah Wesley was the mother of John and

Charles and nine other children. John was her tenth child. While her husband, the Reverend Samuel Wesley, was in prison for debt, she conducted services in her kitchen every Saturday night. When he rebuked her from prison for doing so, she stood her ground, defending, with unanswerable arguments, her right to minister. Though she performed the duties of housekeeper, cook, and washerwoman for her large family, she nevertheless managed to set one hour aside every week for spiritual ministration to each child. *Those hours of ministration laid the foundation for John Wesley's amazing evangelistic career, which historians assert saved England from the French Revolution. They also laid the foundation for the great Methodist Church and for the beautiful hymns of Charles Wesley.*

And it was the need of the world, the multitudes unreached by any church, that resulted in the creation of the Salvation Army by both Catherine and William Booth. Again, quoting Mr. Stead:

> It was Mrs. Booth who made the Army the great instrument that it has been, revealing to the world the capacities and resources of her own sex, and it was Mrs. Booth who, by the warmth of her love and the wealth of her prudence, supplemented the genius of her husband in such a way as to enable him, with her, to do a work for which there is no parallel in our times.[11]

This organization is now functioning in 82 countries, on five continents, and its women officers together with its men officers, preach the Gospel in 106 languages.

This brings to mind another instance of how a woman met the world's need. The coffee and donuts that forever endeared the Salvation Army lassies to the hearts of American men in World War I typified the vision and organizational genius of *Evangeline Booth,* youngest Booth daughter and Commander of the American Salvation Army forces. (In 1934 she was elected General of the World Salvation Army.) At her New York headquarters she gathered together, for a day of prayer and instruction, the leaders of the contingents she was sending abroad to serve the American forces. For this she borrowed "in faith" $25,000.

Concerning that meeting, Evangeline Booth's biographer writes.[12]

> Before the Most High God she called upon them to tell her if any of them had in the heart any motive in leaving the country other than to serve Christ. She looked on the girls in the party and bade them to put away from themselves the arts and coquetries of youth. They were sent forth to love the souls of men as God loved them. Unless self be forgotten, their work would be in vain. If at this final hour of parting, any faltered or felt unfit for the God-given task, let him — let her speak before it was too late. For they held in their hands the honor of the Salvation Army and the glory of Jesus Christ and they were to be examples of His love, willing to lay down their lives if need be, for His sake. They knelt and prayed.

Wherever there is a "glorious company of the Apostles," wrote Evangeline Booth. . . *wherever there is a "goodly fellowship of the prophets," wherever there is a "noble army of martyrs," there will be found the King's Daughters, all radiant within and clothed with glistening robes of righteousness. . . . Upon the scroll of history, stained with . . . blood and tears, you will find the dynasty of sainthood, which women have maintained unbroken. They have been the heroines of home . . . of emancipation . . . of service . . . of sacrifice. If a woman champions a cause, she will fight for it. If she gives, she gives all. If she lives for, she will die for.*

Among her many honors, Evangeline Booth especially treasured the Distinguished Service Medal, conferred by President Wilson, and the Fairfax Medal for Eminent Patriotic Services.

It was World War II that prepared another outstanding woman to preach God's word to the world. *Corrie ten Boom's* faith was tested in Nazi prisons; and in the thirty years since the war ended she has twice circled the world, speaking in more than sixty countries and on every continent. Those who have read her books, *The Hiding Place* and *Tramp for the Lord*[13] are not likely to doubt that God expects women to share his ministry with men. "After that time in prison," said Miss ten Boom, "the entire world became my classroom."

Women whose natural and spiritual talents equip them to meet the world's needs should be encouraged to use them to the fullest. To compel them to waste such treasures in trivial pursuits would be sinful.

Each endowment, each gift, comes from the Father of lights.[14] Jesus told us to invest our talents wisely so that they can increase. He condemned the servant who buried his talent.[15] Would the Lord endow a woman with gifts that could be effectively used to do his work and serve humanity, and then command her not to use them! Jesus also instructed his disciples not to put their light under a bushel, but to let it shine before men.[16] Should women disciples who are called to the ministry put their God-given light under the bushel of male dominance?

A tragic example of what can happen when the need for feminine ministry is denied by a church body is the comment that was made by a young Episcopal priest when he received Communion from the hands of a recently ordained woman priest. As he took the bread he scratched her hand until the blood flowed and muttered that he hoped she would burn in hell.

What a revelation of resistance, resentment, and sex prejudice! Who were the teachers of this young priest that they were unable to perceive the extremities toward which he was drifting in his attitude toward more than fifty percent of the human race? Why could they not detect his spiritual deformity? How could they so blindly ordain such a man? What kind of counsel could even a *man*, with problems in his married life, expect to receive from such a priest? How could he possibly counsel a *woman?* Is it not frightening to contemplate that for the next forty or fifty years this man will be actively playing the part of a ministering priest in some church somewhere? How many others are there who share his views?

And the loftiness of man shall be bowed down, and the haughtiness of men shall be made low: and the Lord alone shall be exalted in that day.[17]

Some years ago, when my brother, William, was a student in Moody Bible Institute in Chicago, one of his professors made some negative remarks about women as ministers. William stood up and reminded the professor about Catherine Booth and the Maréchale. "But there are not many Catherine Booths," the professor observed. To which my brother retorted, "You do not give them the opportunity to become Catherine Booths."

I have heard that the little volume of Scriptural passages entitled *Daily Light*[18] was compiled by two women who chose to remain anonymous. Probably they feared that their offering would be rejected if their sex were known. The thousands of Christians who draw daily inspiration from these lovingly assembled pages might wish to pause, occasionally, to reflect upon the significance of this example of self-sacrifice.

One book unmistakably authored by a woman has taken its place as a classic alongside *Pilgrim's Progress* and *In His Steps.* Entitled *The Christian's Secret of a Happy*

Life,[19] it was written by *Hannah Whitall Smith,* a Philadelphia Quaker, and first printed in 1870. One apparent reason for its popularity is its attitude of optimism and joy. Personal, practical, and inspirational, it has helped both men and women to live richer Christian lives.

There is no superior sex, just as there is no superior race. But we do find superior *individuals,* in both sexes as well as in all races. In some ways a husband may be superior to his wife, and in other ways she may be superior to him. They may be equally outstanding in differing roles. In any case, love creates a beautiful complementary and supplementary union. And if either one is called to the ministry, he or she should receive all the encouragement, assistance, and constructive criticism the other can give.

In 1856 William Booth wrote, "I have just come into the room where my dear little wife is writing — and snatching the paper have read her eulogistic sentiments. I want to say that the very same night she gave me a curtain lecture on my 'block-headism, stupidity, etc.,' and lo, she writes after this fashion! However, she is an increasingly precious treasure to me, despite the occasional dressing down that I come in for."[20]

This attitude of helpfulness and appreciation is often observed in the secular world when professionals in differing careers have married. For centuries it has been proverbial in the wives of ministers. *It should be equally manifest in the husbands of feminine ministers.*

No more beautiful description of the value of feminine ministry was ever expressed than this lament which William Booth delivered beside the open grave of his wife on October 13, 1890:

> If you had had a tree that had grown up in your garden, under your window, which for forty years had been your shadow from the burning sun, whose flowers had been the adornment and beauty of your

life, whose fruit had been almost the very stay of your existence, and the gardener had come along and swung his glittering axe and cut it down before your eyes, I think you would feel as though you had a blank in your life!

If you had had a servant who, for all this long time, had served you without fee or reward, who had administered, for very love, to your health and comfort, and who had suddenly passed away, you would miss that servant!

If you had had a counsellor who in hours — continually occurring — of perplexity and amazement, had ever advised you, and seldom advised wrong; whose advice you had followed and seldom had reason to regret it; and the counsellor, while you are in the same intricate mazes of your existence, had passed away, you would miss that counsellor!

If you had had a friend who had understood your very nature, the rise and fall of your feelings, the bent of your thoughts, and the purpose of your existence; a friend whose communion had ever been pleasant — the most pleasant of all other friends, to whom you had ever turned with satisfaction — and your friend had been taken away, you would feel some sorrow at the loss!

If you had had a mother for your children who had cradled and nursed and trained them for the service of the living God, in which you most delighted; a mother indeed . . . and that darling mother had been taken from your side, you would feel it a sorrow!

If you had had a wife, a sweet love of a wife, who for forty years had never given you real cause for grief; a wife who had stood with you side by side in the battle's front, who had been a comrade to you, ever willing to interpose herself between you and the enemy and ever the strongest when the battle was fiercest, and your beloved one had fallen before your eyes, I am sure there would be some excuse for your sorrow!

Well, my comrades, you can roll all these qualities into one personality and what would be lost in each I have lost, all in one.[21]

Blessed indeed is the wife minister who can speak in the same way about her husband!

THAT ALL MAY SING

Throughout church history there have been women who, even though not permitted to use their prophetic gift by preaching, have expressed it through the writing of hymns.

Never can I forget how worshipfully and feelingly 2,000 Presbyterian ministers sang:

> Be still, my soul: the Lord is on thy side;
> Bear patiently the cross of grief or pain;
> Leave to thy God to order and provide...

The occasion was a meeting of the Prebyterian Pre-Assembly, during the late 1930s, which I had been invited to address on the subject of evangelism. How many of those ministers, I wonder, realized that they were singing words written by a woman (Katharina von Schlegel), set to *Finlandia,* a Sibelius melody, and translated into English by another woman (Jane L. Borthwick). Both of these women also wrote other beautiful hymns.

Whenever people in church, tabernacle, rescue mission or sinking ship (witness the *Titanic*) sing the words: *Nearer my God to Thee, E'en though it be a cross that raiseth me,* they are singing a hymn written by a woman — Sarah F. Adams.

The same applies to such familiar hymns as *I Need Thee Every Hour* (Annie S. Hawks); *Beneath the Cross of Jesus* (Elizabeth Clephane); *Saviour Like a Shepherd Lead Us* (Dorothy Ann Thrupp); *I Love to Tell the Story* (Katherine Hankey); *Jesus Calls Us O'er the Tumult* (Mrs. Cecil Frances Alexander); *Blessed Assurance — This Is My Story, This Is My Song; He Hideth My Soul; I Am Thine, O Lord; Jesus Keep Me Near the Cross; All the Way My Saviour Leads Me,* to name only a few by Fanny J. Crosby.

Among the rousing songs of the Billy Sunday era written by women we find *If Your Heart Keeps Right* (Lizzie De Armond), *Brighten the Corner Where You Are* (Ira Duly Ogden), and *We Have An Anchor* (Priscilla J. Owens).

Concerning the latter, in memory I still hear the ringing voices of great audiences in my Newfoundland meetings as my husband led the fishermen and their families and friends in singing:

> *We have an anchor that keeps the soul*
> *Steadfast and sure, while the billows roll,*
> *Fastened to the Rock which cannot move,*
> *Grounded firm and deep, in the Saviour's love. . .*

A chorus perfectly fitted to their daily experiences on the sea.

Two of the verses read:

> *Will your anchor hold in the storm of life,*
> *When the clouds unfold their wings of strife?*
> *When the strong tides lift, and the cables strain,*
> *Will your anchor drift, or firm remain?*

> *It is safely moored, 'twill the storm withstand,*
> *For 'tis well secured by the Saviour's hand,*
> *And the cables, passed from His Heart to mine,*
> *Can defy the blast, through strength divine.*

Among hymns of challenge written by women we can mention Sallie Hume-Douglas' *Follow the Gleam* and Mary A. Thompson's *O Zion Haste.*

Consider more hymns written by women — hymns of devotion, challenge, patriotism, consecration, and evangelistic appeal, such as *Take my Life and let it be Consecrated, Lord, to Thee; Lord, Speak to Me that I May Speak;* and *True-Hearted Whole-Hearted,* among the many by Frances R. Havergal.

To these we could add Sabine Baring-Gould's *Now the Day is Over;* Harriet Beecher Stowe's *Still Still with Thee* (to music by Mendelssohn); Louise M. R. Stead's *'Tis So Sweet to Trust in Jesus;* Mary Ann Lathbury's *Break Thou the Bread of Life;* Jessie Brown Pound's *The Way of the Cross Leads Home;* Mary A. Baker's *Master, The Tempest is Raging.*

Additional favorites include: Ellen Lakshmi Gareh's *In the Secret of His Presence;* Mrs. C. H. Morris' *Sweet Will of God;* Mary Brown's *I'll Go Where You Want Me To Go;* Lydia Baxter's *Take the Name of Jesus With You;* and Dorothy Guerney's *O Perfect Love, All Human Love Transcending.* Also Mary Duncan's *Jesus, Tender Shepherd, Hear Me;* Jemima Luke's *I Think When I Read that Sweet Story of Old;* Caroline Maria Noel's *At the Name of Jesus Every Knee Shall Bow;* Elizabeth Prentiss' *More Love to Thee, Oh Christ;* Jane C. Bonar's *Fade, Fade Each Earthly Joy, Jesus is Mine;* and various hymns by Christina Georgina Rossetti.

Anyone who will check the hymnbooks and songbooks of every church denomination and those used in Sunday schools, evangelistic meetings, and rescue missions, will be amazed to discover how many of the hymns and songs they contain have been contributed by women.

But most important to the growth of the Church are the songs of appeal written by women — songs that have drawn multitudes to Christ — such as *Pass Me Not O Gentle Saviour,* and *Rescue the Perishing, Jesus is Tenderly Calling Thee Home* by Fanny Crosby; and *We Have Heard* the *Joyful Sound, Jesus Saves* by Priscilla J. Owen.

Just As I Am, the greatest among these, was written by a young woman (and an Episcopalian at that!), Charlotte Elliot. It was a step-by-step account of her own conversion. Indeed it is a perfect portrayal of that experience. This hymn, known the world over, has been used by God to bring thousands into the Kingdom. (Charlotte Elliot also wrote other hymns, among them, *My God, My Father, While I Stray.*)

Another woman, E. Margaret Clarkson, wrote:

So send I you to labor unrewarded . . .
To serve unpaid, unloved, unsought, unknown . . .

The final stanza of this hymn begins:

So send I you to hearts made hard by hatred . . .
To eyes made blind because they will not see . . .

We American citizens might remind ourselves that women gave us our greatest patriotic songs: *America the Beautiful,* Katherine Lee Bates, and *The Battle Hymn of the Republic,* Julia Ward Howe. It was also a woman, Emma Lazarus, who wrote these lines:

> *. . . Give me your tired, your poor,*
> *Your huddled masses yearning to breathe free,*
> *The wretched refuse of your teeming shore.*
> *Send these, the homeless, tempest-tossed to me,*
> *I lift my lamp beside the golden door! . . .*

which are inscribed on the base of the Statue of Liberty.

It seems natural to ask why women who write hymns which bless, inspire, and save, have been forbidden to preach *sermons* which do the same. Should such women be kept quiet in the church?

Chapter Seven

MY WITNESS

It was in a small town called Baarn in Holland. I was six or seven years of age. My mother, who was then Commander in Chief of the Salvation Army in Holland, was combing my long hair, dictating a letter to her secretary, ordering the menu for supper, and sending a telegram to an outpost of the Salvation Army — all at the same time. Thus I was introduced to what it meant to be a woman-warrior in God's army, and I was thrilled.

MY NAME — "VICTORY"

To me it is significant that I was born near L'Arche de Triomphe in Paris, because it symbolized victory. When my mother publicly consecrated me to God (in the Army they did not Christen children) she gave me the name *Victoire*, French for *Victory*.

Shortly afterwards my grandfather sent for my mother, and she took me with her to London. As usual with any event, whether a wedding, a funeral, or the consecration of a baby, William Booth saw my arrival as an opportunity to "cast in the net" and catch many fish for the Lord. A new grandchild! Splendid! "We will have a great meeting in Albert Hall and consecrate her."

"But she *has* been consecrated," demurred my mother.

No matter, she should be well consecrated, and the great meeting was held. But at the crucial moment, as my grandfather held me in his arms, he suddenly realized that he did not know my name. His mind had been occupied

William Booth
1829-1912
Co-founder with Catherine Booth of the Salvation Army

with everything else but me.

"What is the child's name?" he whispered to my mother, who was sitting behind him on the platform.

"Victoire," came the answer.

Although his Army was eventually to encircle the globe, the General was impatient with foreign languages. "Can't you speak English?" he asked in a louder whisper.

"Victoria," Mother answered.

So I was not named after the queen after all, as so many have assumed.

Times without number I have thanked my mother for giving me a name that did not permit me to be a quitter. Through the years I have been train-wrecked, ship-wrecked, preached in a temperature of 110 in the shade and below zero in the winter, preached with blood-poisoning in my arm, preached as long as able before babies were born and as soon afterwards as I could. Numerous times I have risen from a sickbed to preach. Always, I have remembered that my name was "Victory."

From the beginning Father and Mother impressed on us children — five boys and five girls (I was second) — that what mattered most was the Kingdom of God. We would sit on the floor, enthralled by stories of their exploits in the "Holy Warfare" — their deliverance from prison, the battles with hooligans, the conversion of criminals, the wondrously transformed lives of rich and poor, educated and ignorant, statesmen and drunkards. Eight of us became preachers, especially my brother William and myself.

Though our mother was first and foremost a preacher and the great "Maréchale" (so named in France, the country of her adoption), she was nevertheless a wonderful mother, continually caring about everything that concerned us — our hair, our teeth, our eyes, our training in music and in languages. She used to say, pointing her long finger, "If you are not going to live for others I won't spend a penny on your education." A phrase she used, "cumberer of the ground," haunted me for years, and I vowed I would never be one.

Since our family moved from country to country we did not attend public schools. Besides, Mother did not want us influenced by godless children. We had governesses at home — French, Swiss, English, German — who, along with secretaries and household help, usually contributed their services out of respect and appreciation for my parents' ministry. Thus at fourteen years of age I could speak four languages — French (my native tongue), Dutch (my first "sermon" at the age of six was preached in Holland to Dutch children gathered in Mother's kitchen), English, and German. What better preparation could a child have for an international ministry? I learned to think of humanity as one great family. I became, in turn, a French girl, a Dutch girl, a Swiss girl, a Belgian girl, and a German girl, according to the country in which I happened to be living.

When I was twelve years of age (we were still living in Holland), my parents were compelled to sever their connection with the Salvation Army. (See Appendix B) This caused my Mother great agony of soul. Not only was that organization like another child of her parents, but in a very real sense it was *her* child also. She had given it birth in France, Switzerland, Holland, and Belgium. She was the first Booth child to be commissioned by her father, in 1881, to found the Salvation Army in a foreign country — France.

MY MOTHER — THE MARECHALE

Despite her mother's feeling that she was too young, my mother, the second Catherine Booth, known as

"Katie," had first spoken in public at the age of fourteen. Her words "fell with extraordinary power upon the listening crowd," according to a letter from her oldest brother Bramwell, who accompanied her. To reassure his mother he said, "Mother dear, you will have to settle this question with God for she is as surely called and inspired by Him for this work as yourself." By the time her father decided to send her to France, she had preached in many parts of England, with remarkable results. According to her biographer, James Strahan, "the change from an audience of 5000 spellbound hearers in the circus of Leeds to a handful of gibing *ouvriers* in the Belleville quarter of Paris was indeed a clashing antithesis."

When Lady Cairns asked Catherine Booth how she dared to let her beautiful young daughter go to "that wicked city," Paris, Mrs. Booth answered quietly, "You don't know Katie. Her innocence is her strength, and she knows the Lord." As to Katie herself, she said, "Christianity means heroism."

Accompanied by three young women, one of whom, Florence Soper, later married her brother Bramwell, she began her ministry in Belleville, a slum quarter of Paris, the haunt of anarchists, nihilists, and cut-throats. One of her first converts was "the devil's wife." An immense woman who would stand, arms akimbo, in the middle of the hall and start riots with a wink of her eye, she was transformed from the worst troublemaker into the leader of Katie's bodyguard.

The Maréchale's ministry, which began among the lowest of the low in society, ultimately reached the upper class in a hall on the Boulevard des Capucines, where members of the French Senate listened to her, standing with their hats in their hands since there were no remaining seats.

During this time she had accepted an urgent invita-

tion to organize the Army in Switzerland. Her early meetings there were frequently interrupted by hecklers who
started riots, and she was ordered to discontinue them.
Ignoring official warnings, she carried on, fleeing from one
canton to another until the Swiss authorities caught up
with her. She was arrested while conducting a meeting in
a wood.

While imprisoned in Neuchatel, awaiting trial, she
wrote her best known hymn, which, in its English translation, begins:

> *Best Beloved of my soul*
> *I am here alone with Thee*
> *And my prison 'tis a Heaven*
> *Since Thou sharest it with me.*

Katie became the heroine of an historic trial. Refusing the counsel of a lawyer, she chose to defend herself. At
the trial a member of the Grand Council said: "You are a
young woman. It is not in accordance with our ideas and
customs that young women should appear in public. We
are scandalized!"

Her rejoinder was a remarkable defense of women
prophets. I quote:

> Had we sung and danced on your stage we
> would have dressed in a manner very different from
> and much less modest than that in which you see us
> dressed. Members of the Council would have come
> and applauded us. You would have brought your
> wives and daughters to see us. But when women
> come to try and save some of the forty or fifty
> thousand of your miserable, irreligious population
> who never enter any place of worship, then you cry
> out that this is unseemly and immodest. As to our
> aim, we are trying to bring these people who out-
> rage your laws, who fight against God, to the feet of
> Him who alone can change them, to the only hope

that exists for them, the Saviour of the world. We work, we live, we suffer to do this. This is our one object — to bring the world to the great Deliverer, Jesus Christ.

The question of all questions, the question which every intelligent man ought to face, is: What are we to do with the masses? If they are not reached by the power of the Gospel, a day will come when they will turn around against you, occasioning terrible trouble and disorder, and awful will be the consequences. Then, gentlemen, you will have reason to regret your action in this matter. If these disturbers are capable of manifesting such hatred, such rage against citizens who pray to God, they will also be capable of manifesting the same rebellious spirit against any other opinions, or any other law which may not please them.

An article in the *Journal de Geneve* declared:

> *This prosecution at Boudry has an immense political significance in the highest sense of that word, and the decision, whatever it may be, will take its place in the history of Republican rights.*[1]

La Maréchale's cause was won! A great victory for the Salvation Army, it was also a great victory for woman's right to preach, for the cause of religious liberty, and for the Kingdom of God everywhere.

At the height of my mother's career, Frances Willard wrote: "The Maréchale's career already fulfills her father's prophecy that women will, if once left free to their action, develop administrative powers fully equal and oftentimes superior to those of men."[2]

And a devoted friend, the Catholic scholar and translator M. Lassaire, said to her, "God has given you the ear of the nation as it is given only once in a hundred years."[3]

When Katie, La Maréchale, returned to France after her imprisonment and trial in Switzerland, she found herself even more famous than before. Everything she said and did was reported.

On her last preaching tour of Europe, at the age of ninety, my mother was taken by the President of the Swiss Republic to visit the cell where she had been incarcerated.

MY FATHER — A QUAKER SALVATIONIST

As my mother's chief of staff for six years before they were married, in 1887, my father also suffered persecution and imprisonment in Switzerland.

By what means, one must ask, had this aristocratic Quaker from North Ireland been brought into the ranks of the Salvation Army and subjected to such indignities as being stoned, covered with mud, and even condemned to death by the Nihilists under the seal of their Paris headquarters?

Arthur Sydney Clibborn was the second son of James Clibborn, owner of large mills and founder of the model town of Bessbrook in which there was no smoking, no alcohol, no gambling, and where every home had a little garden. The Clibborns were descended from seven of the twenty-five barons who compelled King John to affix his seal to the Magna Carta in 1215 (see Appendix F), and also from Barclay of Ury, hero of one of Whittier's poems. When Arthur first came into contact with the Salvation Army he exclaimed, "Here is primitive Quakerism, primitive Wesleyanism, primitive Christianity!"

James, the eldest son, had migrated to Canada. The youngest, Percy, had been lured to America by the gold rush. Arthur, the only one who remained at home, was the center of his father's hopes and the natural successor to his business. But Arthur's interest was aroused by a letter from Catherine Booth, published in a London newspaper, in which she indicated that she was seeking young, educated, French-speaking men and women to assist her daughter in Paris. Arthur, who spoke fluent French and German, felt this letter to be a call to him from God. Even though he dreaded disappointing his father, he knew that he had no other choice. Summoning all of his courage, he told his father about this unusual conviction.

James Clibborn bowed his head. After a moment of silence he said, "Dost thee say, my son, that this is God's call to thee?"

"Yes, my Father."

"Then, my Son, I have nothing to say."

This also was heroism, because in those days the Salvation Army was despised as belonging to the lowest element of society.

My maternal grandfather is honored all over the world, but I also feel proud of my paternal grandfather for this noble act of unquestioning personal sacrifice.

My father was a man of great physical and moral courage. He received a medal from the French President for saving a man from drowning. In the Salvation Army's early days of conflict he was the bravest of the brave and often endangered his life to protect the Maréchale and her comrades.

It was to be expected that my parents' separation from the Salvation Army would be a shock to all their followers and admirers throughout Europe. No one could understand, and my parents could not explain. There followed for our family a time of great suffering, poverty, and trial. My father became ill unto death. He was saved by the devoted nursing of our faithful Adele, who had joined our household when only a peasant girl of sixteen and when I was a two-year-old baby. She stood by us throughout the years, refusing any pay and sharing all the ups and downs and the many crises of the family. She outlived both my father and my mother.

The deep spiritual experiences, the insights, the knowledge acquired through the trials and sufferings of my parents during that dark period (from my twelfth to my eighteenth years) profoundly contributed to and enriched my future ministry. (See Appendix B)

We were again living in France. When I was fourteen I remember throwing myself on my knees and telling God I was willing to die if he would only restore a ministry to my mother. Soon afterward she received invitations from churches in England to conduct preaching missions. Thus began for her a world ministry in evangelism that would not have been hers had she remained in the Army.

DIVINE VISITATION

It was also when I was fourteen that I first experienced a visitation from the Holy Spirit. I was alone in my room. It was suddenly filled with the presence of God, and I knew that I was called. Quite independently of my grandmother and my mother, I knew in my heart that I was called, and from that day to this I have never sought for my ministry the consent or approval of man.

Not long afterward I was present when my mother visited W. T. Stead (the lifelong friend and supporter of the Booths) in England. I well remember his shining blue eyes and his friendly smile as he put his hand on my knee and said, "My child, you would make a wonderful medium." (Mr. Stead had become a convinced spiritualist.) "Mr. Stead," I replied, "I want to be a medium for only one spirit, and that is the Holy Spirit of God."

On the day of my visitation I had made an inventory of the gifts I could offer to God. These included music and languages, to which later would be added public speaking and drama. I made a vow that I would never use any gift or talent, present or future, for any other purpose than the service and glory of God.

I had received a music scholarship to study at the Paris Conservatoire after one of their officials heard me play some little dances I had composed on the piano. Once, I remember well, my father offered me a shilling if I would compose a melody for one of his hymns. (Both of my parents had beautiful voices and wrote many hymns, some of which are still famous throughout Europe.) A shilling seemed like a fortune to me. We children never had any spending money. "Oh Father, I would love to do it," I told him, "but I don't want the shilling." Yet try as I might, for a number of years, I could not compose religious music. Eventually, however, God granted me the gift, and since then I have composed close to one hundred hymns and sacred songs. I have also written three plays and presented them as mono-dramas.

Four years were all I had of "formal" education, in a college in St. Cloud outside Paris. For a short while I also attended the Sorbonne in Paris. Meanwhile, I continued my piano studies.

The star in the dark night of those years was my hope to assist my mother in her ministry. This hope was realized when I was eighteen and graduated with a Brevet Elementaire allowing me to teach in French primary schools. By that time the family had moved to England, and to my great joy, I joined my mother. Thus began my training in the ministry. Words could never express the value to my future of the few years spent assisting my mother.

From my father I learned theology. From my mother I learned the art of preaching and how to win souls. I conducted her aftermeetings, her prayer meetings, trained the choirs, and accompanied the singing of the congregation on the piano. We had only the printed lyrics. I carried more than three hundred tunes in my head and

Victoria Booth-Clibborn
called to the Ministry.

*A Sacred Arts International
Photograph*

Arthur Sydney Booth-Clibborn
1855-1939

could transpose in any key. Mother would call down from
the platform, "Too high" or "Too low."

FIRST PREACHING EXPERIENCE

My first experience in pulpit preaching constitutes a
landmark in my ministry. It was in Scotland. Mother called
me and said, "Darling, I am not able to preach tonight.
You will have to go in my stead." (My mother believed in
teaching a child to swim by throwing it in the water.) It
never occurred to me to demur. I was a soldier in God's
Army and Mother was my captain.

All the way in the bus going to the town where I
was to preach, it seemed that a thousand little devils yelled
in my heart, "It's not fair. You haven't had a chance to
prepare. You can't do it. You can't! You can't!" My
mother's companion and secretary who was appointed to
accompany me, kept grumbling by my side, "It's ridi-
culous. How can you take the Maréchale's place? The
people will be so disappointed."

We arrived at the church. The distinguished minister
welcomed us most graciously, but I could see his face fall
when he was told that I was to preach in Mother's place.
Never was I so grateful for preliminaries, hymns, and the
custom of kneeling for prayers. On my knees I cried to
God, "Lord you know I can't." The answer came in a flash.
"You can't, my Child, but I can." I rose from my knees,
went forward to the pulpit, opened the Bible, and
preached.

When, at the end of the service, the minister and the
people thanked me warmly, I knew that it was the Holy
Spirit, not I, who had brought the message. In a short
while I was invited to conduct two preaching missions on
my own.

"A Victory girl never says I can't" was one of the slogans of the Victory Clubs which, as a result of my own experience, I organized soon after coming to America in 1913. I was twenty-three years old. These clubs were for girls of all denominations and races between the ages of fourteen and twenty-three, who were willing to do anything for Christ — visit the poor, testify in public, sing in nursing homes — just anything. Wherever I conducted a campaign I founded a Victory Club. The largest was in the city of St. Johns, Newfoundland. It numbered one hundred members. A scholarly minister who was quite skeptical concerning the club, asked to attend and was spiritually changed as a result.

One of my first preaching missions in America was conducted in the Parish Hall of St. Luke's High Episcopal Church in Evanston, Illinois. People of every denomination, including Roman Catholic and also some of the Jewish faith, came even from Chicago to these meetings. The Episcopal sisters in their robes attended. And every night the Altar was filled with penitents and with those committing their lives to Christ.

One morning as I arrived at the church office I found Father George Craig Stewart, the young rector, pacing the floor in a great state of excitement. The moment he saw me he pointed his finger and exclaimed, "Now I know where you belong in the divine plan. You are a *prophetess.*" (I was tempted to smile but didn't.)

Being very orderly in his thinking, he had sought to find intellectual justification for his act of inviting me, a young woman, non-Episcopal and unordained, to conduct a preaching mission in his very exclusive church. It was unorthodox, to say the least. Now he had suddenly found Scriptural authority and backing. Are not prophetesses mentioned in the Scriptures? His joy knew no bounds. "You are a *prophetess!*" That settled it. Many years later

George Craig Stewart became the Bishop of the Diocese of Chicago. When I visited him he put his hand on mine and said, "What our people need, Mrs. Demarest, is to be converted."

MARRIAGE AND MINISTRY

In 1918 I married Cornelius Agnew Demarest, organist and choir master of the Second Presbyterian Church in Louisville, Kentucky. He said he fell in love with me when I was mounting the steps to the pulpit of his church, dressed in my Alice-blue preaching gown with the little white collar, wearing my silver Cross and with the Bible in my hand. "You made me think of Joan of Arc," he told me later. And with pride he pulled out all the stops on the organ for the opening hymn of the service.

This is how it happened. I had been the only woman and the youngest speaker that afternoon at a convention of the Purity Federation held in the Palace Theater. When it was announced, after my talk, that I would speak shortly afterwards in the Y.W.C.A., half of the audience left the theater to head for the Y, even though several prominent men were still to speak. In a very little while an overflow crowd was being turned away from the Y, which was across the street from the Presbyterian Church. At this point, Mr. Demarest, who had attended the meeting in the Palace Theater, burst in on the church elders, who were in session, and requested that I be invited to deliver my address in the church instead. When the elders gasped, my future husband exclaimed, "What is a church for? Is it not for the preaching of the Gospel?" And then he added, "There is no time for discussion. If you gentlemen refuse my request I will resign my position as organist and choir master." The church doors were promptly opened and the church was immediately filled to the top gallery. Agnew's courage impressed me greatly. I said to myself, "I like that. He has guts."

I was sitting sewing in the garden of my Chicago home when a friend called. "Victoria, let me look at you," she said. "Do you mean to tell me that you are going to marry a widower with two little boys and expect to go on preaching! How can you do this?" "I don't know," I answered. "I only know that it is God's will that I marry Mr. Demarest and be a good mother to his boys (eight and ten years old) and to any children that God will give me. I also know it is God's will for me to go on preaching. Since it is His will it is His business, and He will make it possible." And He did!

"A twentieth-century husband" was the description given to Mr. Demarest by one of my dearest friends and enthusiastic supporters, the Reverend Madeline Southard (founder in 1920 of the American Association of Women Ministers — today the International Association of Women Ministers — my mother was a charter member). Miss Southard was impressed by my husband's perfect collaboration in my work. He was a strong champion of women in the ministry. One time, in response to a letter of mine telling him I had met with opposition, he wrote:

> So, someone objected to a woman preaching! I would like to ask that man who commits at least ninety-five percent of the murders . . . who are the leaders in the white slave traffic . . . who are ninety-five percent of the grafters in politics . . . who are ninety-five percent of the gangsters? The vast majority of women are law-abiding citizens— and the mainstay of the Church and of Christianity. And where would public education be without the public school teachers, most of whom are women? Since very evidently women are the backbone of morality, good citizenship, education, and religion, I would like to ask that man why they should not preach? What has woman done to be thus despised? If the

right to preach were given to the sex most deserving it on the basis of good behavior and loyalty to the Church, surely it would be given to women. *Some day you must write that book on women's ministry started once — and give it to the men HOT!*

Though he listened to me thousands of times during the years while he was manager, music director, and co-worker in every way in our evangelistic campaigns, my husband said that he never tired of my preaching. "It is always new and fresh," he said. "To see you and hear you in the pulpit is a true bit of heaven," he once wrote to me. "You are unequalled by man or woman. When you are preaching you are not my wife, my love, not even the mother of my children — you are a thing apart — you are God's Voice!" I treasure the Bible he gave to me in 1944. In it he wrote: "To my life companion, whose God-given power to expound Scripture with understanding and simplicity as well as with love and winsomeness is equalled by few and exceeded by none."

Just as it was natural for me to be the leader in our evangelistic work, so it was natural for Agnew to be the follower. This did not take away from my femininity or from his masculinity. My dear husband knew well how mentally, physically, emotionally, and spiritually exhausting my work could be. He appreciated its value because he constantly witnessed its joyful results. Many times he told me that he felt it to be his calling to share in this ministry by relieving me as much as possible from avoidable stress and strain. He felt no hesitation about changing a baby, cooking a meal (he loved to cook), or attending to any chores I could not take care of. As for me, I was akin to my grandmother who wrote her parents, "Indeed, I feel quite at home on the platform, far more than I do in the kitchen!"[4] My husband and I shared responsibilities, whether for the home, music, ministry, or the rearing of our children. That, to my mind, is a true marriage.

Why should there be any demarcation between man's work and woman's work? Ability and need should direct the choice of the task. (Howard Brunner said, "It is absolutely impossible to put down in black and white, as a universal rule, which spheres of activity 'belong' to women and which do not. *This can only become clear through experience;* and for this experience the field must be thrown open.") Where there are children, parents share responsibility for rearing them — and this responsibility is spiritual as well as material. In fact, the Bible heavily emphasizes the spiritual responsibility of the father.

Nevertheless, although I believe in the equality of the sexes, there is a sense in which the husband is the "head" of the wife no matter how mature or educated she may be. She needs him to lean on, to depend on. She needs him to give her a sense of emotional security. Her femininity calls for him to be head.

Furthermore, unless the husband can feel that his wife depends on him for help, he will lose his sense of dignity and manhood, and his sense of responsibility will suffer. This will react on the wife, who may then find that she has become a mere sex object in his eyes, and she will feel degraded and lose her own sense of dignity and personal worth.

One thing is certain in a true marriage. There must be mutual respect. Love is impossible without it. Pity, yes. Physical attraction, yes. But not love.

Of course, my husband and I had our share of conflicts. These are unavoidable in the marriage of two equally strong personalities. We had conflicts about music, about helpers, about management, about the children. Human love is not enough to make a marriage succeed. The Grace of God is needed. In our marriage, Christ was supreme, and we mutually wanted to please him. That was our meeting ground.

In the battle of the sexes there is a great danger that each sex will destroy the other by seeking first its own rights. Christ gives us the solution, viz., "the washing of the feet," symbolizing service. As his followers we must consider ourselves as first being "ministers to each other." Husband and wife should glory in ministering to each other's needs — sexual, emotional, intellectual, as well as material. This constitutes true marriage. Paul was right in saying that man was for woman and woman for man.

MOTHERHOOD AND MINISTRY

Motherhood fitted into my life as perfectly as did the ministry. My happiest moments, when I felt most "at home," were when I was clasping one of my newborn babies in my arms or when I was in the pulpit preaching the Word of God. Thus I was fulfilling both my physical and my spiritual destiny.

Never did a baby of mine interfere with my ministry. People used to say of my babies that they were made to order. I would put them on pillows on the floor of the vestry with their bottles while I went to the pulpit to preach, and they would gurgle happily.

In one of her many speeches, Maud Ballington Booth, who, in addition to raising two children of her own, was known as "Little Mother" by the thousands of American prisoners whom she assisted in her chosen work, the rehabilitation of ex-convicts, declared:

> I believe that we can hold our darlings with a tighter grasp, that they are safer, and that they shall be greatly blessed by the fact that we take also into our hearts the motherless, unloved ones whom we can help and comfort . . .[5]

She believed that the feeling of motherhood, ex-

THE DEMARESTS — *standing:* Cornelius and John. *Seated:* Agnew, Arthur, David, Danny, Victoria. *On the floor:* Vicky.

—*Photo by Moffett*

pressed in love and care, was a reflection of God's love for his children, and that the more it comprehended, the greater its likeness to the Divine.

As for myself, the joys and sorrows of motherhood have all been mine. I bore six children — and lost four sons, one of them my eldest step-son, John.

I have already mentioned the two little boys, Cornelius and John, who became my sons when I married my husband. The six children born to me were Eric Booth, Victoria Beatrice, Arthur Sidney, David Livingstone, Daniel Noble, and, in my forties, Evangeline Catherine.

My firstborn, called Eric after my brother who introduced Agnew to me and married us, died when he was three days old (as a result of mishandling at birth). He was so beautiful that I had his picture taken on his father's lap. I tell the story in my autobiography.

Daniel Noble, who died when he was two and a half years old, was sunshine incarnate. He too was a beautiful child, and so dramatic and musical that he would stand up in his high chair and vigorously conduct the singing, "Et it go, et it go . . ." ("Let it go, let it go! What has God not brought you through? He will work it out for you." This was a chorus composed by my brother William.) He faded away in my arms. He could not hold any food. We only knew the cause of his death after an autopsy was performed — encephalitis meningitis! His death led to my writing of "Shade of His Hand," a book which has brought comfort to thousands of aching hearts.

David Livingstone lost his life when only twenty years old. Well do I remember the joy and pride of my tall, handsome David as he escorted me to and from the platform in Greenville, Tennessee, where I delivered an address for the Gold Star Mothers. Little did I suspect that soon I myself would be one of them. My son was accidentally shot by our own men on the island of Guam on

December 3, 1944, the year before the Armistice in World War II. They did not suffficiently raise their sights in practice! David was a pharmacist's mate in the United States Marine Corps. "I don't want to kill, Mother," he had said. "I want to heal." God answered his prayer. He never killed anyone. If he had died on God's battlefield, to which I had dedicated him, it would have been much easier to bear. With memory's eye I still see his beautiful hands that could carve lovely things, and I hear his gorgeous singing voice. His commanding officer wrote me a beautiful tribute to his character. It was shortly after his death that I organized the World Association of Mothers for Peace.

I lost a fourth son when John died in 1967. The shock of a fire which burned his home and all his possessions caused heart failure. I heard the news in Italy where I was visiting my youngest daughter Evangeline. He was a loyal champion of my ministry to the end of his life.

And now my living children. Cornelius, eight years old when I married his father, has remained very close to me. He has a delightful family and lives in Lexington, Kentucky.

My very gifted daughter, Victoria, married an Episcopal clergyman, the Reverend Claxton Monro, and has assisted him in the remarkable work for which he has become famous — encouraging Christian laymen to become leaders in every Church activity. On several occasions I preached in his church at his invitation. He and Vicki are parents of three daughters and one son.

Arthur Sidney, my eldest son, had planned to become a minister, but circumstances intervened. A broker in New York, he is the father of a son and a daughter. I have before me a sweet letter expressing his love. His son, David Michael Demarest, a commercial artist, has designed the covers for my books.

Evangeline, my youngest, who is an opera singer (I call her my "nightingale"), lives with me now. Feeling I should not be allowed to live alone any longer, she came home from Italy, and her musical knowledge and gifts have helped me as I have continued to compose hymns and songs.

The occasions when I had to be away from my children when they were young were the hardest aspect of my work. No one but a mother can understand the suffering involved in being deprived of her children during their growing years, and, even worse, fearing the children themselves might suffer. I hurried home to them as often as possible. Fortunately, I had devoted helpers at home, and we exchanged daily letters. Their letters were my meat and drink. They gave me detailed news, reported the children's cute sayings and doings, their achievements, their mischief, and gave me a minute account of their health.

In a letter to my husband, written after we had lost our home because of the great depression, I said:

A child needs love just as flowers need the sunshine. God has given the child to the mother and the mother to the child. You know how I have fought all these years to keep up the home and to spend as much time as possible with my children. Before I married you, Darling, I asked God to make the seemingly impossible possible, to help me to do my duty by His work, to which I had given my life, and also to be a good wife to my husband and a good mother to my children. Had I not believed that he would somehow answer that prayer, I never would have married . . .

It is natural for Baby to want me. All I can do is to match her feelings tenderly and wisely, letting her know that I want her as much as she wants me. We have kept our children at home even though I have had to leave them. I have returned home every four or five weeks. Now if Eve lives too much with other people she may not have the spiritual life and sensitivity and power that I desire her to have. I must practice what I have preached to thousands of women and mothers in my lectures. I have prayed and prayed with tears, and I have fought like a tigress (and I intend to keep on fighting) that my children may never turn on religion and say that it robbed them of their mother.

STRESS AND STRAIN

One often expressed objection to ordaining women to the ministry is that the work involved is considered too strenuous. Man still regards woman as the "weaker sex." My own experience has proved this to be absolutely false. The evangelistic ministry is far more strenuous than even that of regular church ministry. With the help of my devoted husband and secretaries, I sometimes had to conduct campaigns from my bed, rising at night to preach. Doctors used to say, "You do the work of ten men, Mrs. Demarest, and if you continue this you won't live long." But I am still alive and running!

At the end of nightly meetings, in union campaigns lasting three or four weeks, after I had preached for most of an hour and was doing counselling and dealing with needy souls, ministers would come to me, one by one, and say, "Mrs. Demarest, will you please excuse me? I can stay no longer for I am very tired." This used to make me smile. Here I was, sometimes big with child, often working on until 1:00 in the morning. But the male ministers had to go home!

(I should mention that when expecting a child I was always very careful of my appearance in order to avoid embarrassment to others as well as to myself. I knew how to dress, and my long blue preaching gowns were becoming as well as a good disguise. If people guessed they only respected me the more.)

Women have proven that they have more staying power than men. They can endure emotional stress far better, and statistics show that they live longer. Besides, it should not be forgotten that in the ministry, whether it be evangelistic or pastoral, both men and women have divine resources available. I know from personal experience that I could never have done the work I have been able to accomplish had it not been for the divine strength given me.

During the terrible depression, when we had no home, the children were scattered, and I had to go on *alone* accepting any invitation I could for a preaching mission, even if it were in an abandoned store, my dear husband wrote me as follows:

> *I have just come from St. Thomas' Church. When I thought of you preaching alone tonight my heart sank. But these are times of testing. It seems to me that our lives have been directed in such a way as to compel us to abandon confidence in the flesh, in ways and means, in ourselves — in everything but God!*
>
> *I am glad you can speak "The Wonders of His Grace." If you convict and win even one soul you will do more than Dr. B. did this morning in that immense church crowded to the doors. What opportunities are often wasted! I am comforted by the thought of your superb heroism, your dauntless courage, your perseverance in spite of all Hell!*
>
> *Though undoubtedly the whole course of my life was changed when I met and married you, I would not return to the "old" for anything; for it is because I have known and loved you that my life has been enriched. I have not only learned the joys of life and love but I have also experienced spiritual joys through my fellowship with you and your life of service.*
>
> *As time goes on I feel more and more that my*

Victoria Booth Demarest as Mary Magdalene
Massey Hall, Toronto, Canada — 1933

—Photo by W. A. Pidduck, Toronto

A Sacred Arts International Photograph

duty to God is to be on my knees in gratitude for
His guidance in bringing us together and putting
your hand in mine and my arm around you!

DRAMA AS A VEHICLE OF MINISTRY

And now to speak of another feature of my ministry
— namely, drama.

Even though my sometimes unconventional ideas
might startle my dignified husband, he always gave me his
loyal support. In 1933, when I was conducting my twelfth
campaign in Toronto, Canada, I said to him, "I'm going to
throw a bomb in the camp!"

"What now?" he responded with suspended en-
thusiasm.

"I am going to give my play, *The Empty House*, in
Massey Hall. And we will fill it."

He gasped. Massey Hall seated 3000, and the stage
could accommodate 300.

"We'll reach everybody," I continued. "The students,
the rich, the poor, the social sets — everybody!" And we
did. The hall was packed.

For years I had wanted to demonstrate that the
dramatic medium used by Jesus in his parables was a
powerful means of conveying the Gospel to masses of
people. I had never acted. But I had written a dramatiza-
tion of the parable about the devils who took possession of
the House of Man because it was empty, though swept and
garnished.[6] And I had given readings of it for enthusiastic
friends. It was this drama, entitled *The Empty House*,
which I now proposed to perform.

Our staging was simple. The suggestion of a wood
against a black backdrop. In one corner the House of Man
with a single window, lit from within. I played the parts
of seven different devils, changing my costume only when
I exchanged my devil robe and turban (deep red-gold) for

a white robe in which I portrayed Mary Magdalene, who appeared at the end and ordered the devils back before giving her witness — that out of her the Lord had cast seven devils.

But while I was preparing this presentation, as I was memorizing my parts, I was suddenly assailed by the most fearful doubts. How could I, a vessel of the Lord, lend my body to the portrayal of devils! That I would also be Mary Magdalene did not console me. For days I was in a state of torment, and I knew our production would be a ghastly fiasco unless I could be delivered. As the scheduled date drew near I threw myself to my knees in desperation. "Oh, God, help me!" I cried. "Am I making a terrible mistake?"

In a flash the answer came. "Who knows better than I the power of evil and the way of deliverance!"

I jumped to my feet. "Lord!" I exclaimed, "I will portray those devils so vividly that the people will tremble!" From that moment I had complete confidence of victory.

The play was a sensation. The four leading dramatic critics occupied front seats and wrote enthusiastic reports. Best of all, my objective was accomplished. People were made to realize the futility of mere reformation, exemplified by the sweeping and the garnishing, because the heart of man is still the target of evil forces unless it is occupied by the spirit of Christ.

"I was never conscious of you as Mrs. Demarest," wrote the Reverend James Little, D.D., Westminster United Church of Canada, Toronto. Calling it "one of the most outstanding events of my life," he commented, "In this way you reach some not reached by the more abstract way of preaching."

"As a religious lesson it was deeply impressive," wrote Lawrence Mason in the Toronto *Globe* and *Mail.* "It was an extraordinary achievement."

Subsequently I repeated the production a number of times by request, both in Canada and in the United States. "The potency and uniqueness of this play provide a new medium for imparting spiritual truth," wrote the Director of the Department of Sacred Arts at the Chicago Conservatory. To which the Executive Secretary of the New York Episcopal Actors' Guild added, "The world needs spiritual productions such as yours."

ORDINATION

Twice during the long years of my evangelistic ministry I was offered ordination — once by the Baptist and another time by the Methodist denominations. But I did not accept for several reasons. First, I did not want to be honored as an "exception." I did not want a recognition that was withheld from other consecrated and deserving women. Second, in my lectures to women and the special counselling connected with them I thought the women would feel that, as a laywoman, I was one of them and therefore better able to enter into their lives.

However, when ordination was again offered me in 1949, this time by the Congregational denomination, I felt distinctly led to accept. Let me explain how this developed. It was a slow process which evolved from roots that had been planted eighteen years earlier.

In 1931 I had been the only evangelist (and a woman at that) ever to be engaged to conduct Union Evangelistic Campaigns in every borough of greater New York, under the auspices of the Federal Council of Churches (now the National Council of Churches). These lasted throughout the whole winter of 1931-32. In each borough, churches of all Protestant denominations united for services in a church of a different denomination. In this way all denominations had equal recognition. For instance, in Flushing the churches united in a Lutheran Church. In Staten Island they met in the Church of the Reformed.

To say that the winter's work was exhausting is to put it mildly. Often the cooperation of ministers was just on paper, and the burden fell on me. This was during the depression years when the spiritual needs of the people were even more overwhelming than their financial needs. On one occasion, when I entered the Cathedral of St. Peter's on Fifth Avenue to pray, a young man fainted at my feet because he was so weak from hunger. I assisted him as best I could, and when he could walk again, I took him to a nearby restaurant for a meal — and for spiritual comfort as well, for which he was extremely grateful.

Being away from the children for so long made the winter even harder. But the Lord gave me the strength, and during those months, I composed the hymn which contains the lines: "His grace is sufficient for me. His strength is made perfect in weakness." (That hymn has gone around the world.)

Following these campaigns I was invited to give a series of addresses in Town Hall which were attended by the New York elite. In addition, I held several "drawing room meetings" in the homes of wealthy, socially prominent New Yorkers. Among them were Mrs. Stephen Baker, wife of the President of Chase-Manhattan Bank; Mrs. Simeon B. Chapin, and Mme. Louise Homer. (One night I also addressed the bums and the drunks in the Bowery, and lo! a number of my friends from the other part of town requested and received permission to attend. The first to be converted that night was a beautiful, young Episcopalian woman.)

In Manhattan the campaign had centered in the Christ Church Methodist, of which Ralph W. Sockman, D.D., LL.D., was pastor, and also in the West End Presbyterian Church, where A. Edwin Keigwin, D.D., LL.D., was pastor. Both of these ministers became personal friends and champions of my ministry.

From that time on Dr. Keigwin had me preach for him whenever I came through New York. (From 1925 to 1936 we made our home in Norfolk, Virginia.) He was most desirous that I be ordained by the Presbyterian Church. He even had me assist him in administering the Lord's Supper. When I said to him, "Dr. Keigwin, you will get into trouble with your denomination," he replied, "As far as I am concerned, Victoria, you *are* ordained."

In 1948, however, the Presbyterian General Assembly turned down Ouverture D on the ordination of women. (By then we had moved from Virginia to New York City.) So when Alfred Grant Walton, D.D., LL.D. — in whose church, the Flatbush-Tompkins Congregational Church in Brooklyn, I had preached — offered to propose me for ordination by his denomination, Dr. Keigwin urged me to accept. This I did, on the condition that he be invited to participate. As a result, it was he who offered the Ordination Prayer. For years he had prayed to live to see me ordained. His prayer was answered. He died the following year, in his late seventies.

Ordination is a unique experience, a solemn occasion for any minister. My own ordination by the Congregational Church took place on May 29, 1949, in the Broadway Tabernacle, New York City.

The service was, for me, a beautiful event. I was heartened by the participation of many friends and loved ones, and especially happy to have my husband at the organ. As a prelude he played five of my hymns and songs, and the large congregation sang the following hymn, which I composed especially for the occasion.

THE LIFE OF CHRIST

"The life was the light of men." John 1:4

Forth from the Church of Christ doth flow
His life in glorious streams
That cleanse, renew and make to glow
The souls that He redeems.
The One Whom we adore and love
Is not a buried Lord —
He lives, not just in realms above
But in His Church and Word.

His life doth make the coward strong.
It makes the unclean pure;
His life doth conquer ev'ry wrong,
And makes salvation sure.
His life — unchanging through the years
Renews our youth and joy;
It drives away our griefs and fears
And gives us brave employ.

Thy life, O Christ, is light of men
Dispelling all our gloom;
Its pow'r is far beyond our ken.
It conquers death and doom.
Oh quicken me, Thou life divine,
Renewing all my frame;
For soul and body, all are Thine.
To glorify Thy Name.

The officiating clergy were my friends in the ministry. William Walter Rockwell, who tutored me in preparation for ordination, was Librarian Emeritus of Union Theological Seminary, New York. Donald Strickler was then Executive Secretary of the New York City Congregational Church Association. Lee Vaughn Barker was Assistant Pastor of Broadway Tabernacle. They were joined by the great scholar and preacher, Gaius Glen Atkins. Alfred Grant Walton presented me for ordination, and the Ordination Prayer was offered by Edwin Keigwin.

The ceremony in itself reflected a growing ecumenical spirit in the Protestant fellowship, and this filled me with joy.

Among the many letters received after the ordination, I treasured one in particular from Dr. Frederick W. Evans, Moderator of the 58th General Assembly of the Presbyterian Church, U.S.A. He wrote: "Long before this ordination on earth you had another, namely that spoken of in John 15:16 — 'I have chosen you and ordained you that you should go and bring forth fruit.'"

Though ordained by the Congregational Fellowship, it was understood that I would not take a pastorate. This would have compelled me to abandon the evangelistic and ecumenical ministry to which I had been called and to which I had devoted all my life. Thus I had to forego whatever financial security a pastorate would have offered.

It should be noted that my ministry never had permanent financial backing or support. No endowment. No organization. No church. Nothing but God. From the beginning I accepted invitations as they came and supported myself. Later my husband and I supported the family on the thank offerings we received from grateful people in our campaigns. It was an uphill fight all the way.

Moreover, through all my years of ministry, I had to combat prejudice, criticism, and opposition. Sad to say, this came not from the world but from "religious" people. I found that even leaders in the Lord's work were reluctant to acknowledge the spiritual effectiveness of a woman's ministry.

Victoria Booth Demarest
— in her forties
"I know from personal
experience that I could never have
done the work I have been able to
accomplish had it not been for
the divine strength given me."
— VBD

Sacred Arts International

Photographs

The Reverend
Victoria Booth Demarest
— in her fifties
"Long before this ordination on
earth you had another, namely
that spoken of in John 15:16 —
'I have chosen you and ordained
you that you should go and
bring forth fruit.' "
— Dr. F. W. Evans

Frank Buchman, who created the Oxford Movement, which later became "Moral Rearmament" and spread throughout the world, waited until my mother had died before he admitted in the press that it was in her meetings, during a convention in Keswick, north of England, that he experienced the revolutionary change which sparked this unusual and effective world ministry.

This attitude was illustrated many times in my life. On one occasion the leader of an international evangelistic movement recognized me in a great meeting and introduced me by name but forebore to tell the audience that, as an unbelieving and scoffing young man, he had been converted in one of my meetings in Canada. Had I been a man, he would have been proud to acknowledge his debt to me. This would be a laughing matter were it not so foolish and sad. On another occasion, in a great evangelistic convention in Chicago, the Negro preachers in the audience were publicly invited to come to the platform. But I was not invited, though I had preached in several churches in the city and was sitting, dressed in my preaching robe, on the front row of the auditorium.

Nevertheless, I have had many loyal male friends and enthusiastic endorsers of my ministry who were leaders in their denominations. These included Bishops of the Methodist and the Episcopal churches.

KIRCHENTAG

A landmark in my ministry was my experience in delivering an address to an audience of 20,000 in the great open-air ampitheater called the *Waldbühne* in Berlin, in 1951. I was one of the speakers for "Kirchentag" (German Evangelical Congress of Laity). The people had come from all over Germany — on horseback, in wagons, on foot, in every possible type of conveyance, sacrificially spending what little money they had in order to attend this five-day Congress. They would stand or sit on the floor, in the tents or in the parks outside, listening to addresses broadcast from several of the buildings over the loudspeakers.

An educated young man had been appointed to be my interpreter. He had been one of the Hitler youths in the early years of the war, but was now thoroughly disillusioned. Shortly before I was to give my address I said to him, "Christopher, do you believe in miracles?" He looked at me in astonishment. I continued, "These days spent in Berlin, seeing the terrible and awesome destruction of the city, and talking to the people — waiters, taxi drivers, grieving mothers, young people, everybody — I have been deeply moved. I would like to speak to them in their own language. I know you have translated my address into German and that I haven't spoken German for practically thirty years, but I don't want anything to stand between their hearts and mine. God has put it in my heart to speak to them directly in their own language, and he will enable me to do it. Will you pray with me?" We prayed together.

I was the last speaker on the program. There was no microphone. The sounding board in the open air was a very high perpendicular rock directly behind the speaker's stand. Many wonderful speakers had preceded me. One was an African, black as coal, whose face shone with the glory of God. Before my turn came it began to rain. My heart filled with dismay. I feared that the people would leave. But none moved. Instead, they held newspapers over their heads. I was wearing my preaching gown, and I suppose that the fact that a woman would be the final speaker intrigued them.

When my turn came I had no fear. I delivered my message with power and confidence. Time and again I was interrupted with applause, and especially when I said that I hoped there would be a Kirchentag in every country so that Christians of all church affiliations could come together. And again when I said that, as a mother who had lost a son in the dreadful war, I could enter into their suffering. The biggest applause, however, followed my statement that there was only ONE Church, and that this Church could not be destroyed by bombs. The real Church, I said, the body of Christ, was the heart of every "believer." "*Du* bist die Kirche," I said, pointing to them. "Du und du und du." (You are the Church. You and you and you.)

At the end of my address, I was amazed to see people from all directions running down the steps of the ampitheater and coming towards me. With tears they exclaimed, "Thank you, thank you. Come again. We need you." One woman especially touched my heart. She kissed my gown and tearfully said, "Du bist eine Mutter, du bist eine Mutter. Du kanst verstanden." (*You are a mother. You can understand.*)

I couldn't get away. Christopher had to force an opening for me. When I reached the top of the ampitheater the buses had all left, and when I sat in the car of a lady who offered to take me to my hotel, the people surrounded the car. With tears running down their faces they burst into the beautiful German hymn, "Ich bete an die Macht der Liebe." (*I pray to Thee, great power of love.*) I was moved to tears.

As we drove away I turned to a boy in the car and asked, "How was my German?" He replied, his face shining, "Es war ausgezeichnet." This could be translated into several American words — such as "excellent," "stupendous," "marvelous!" I knew that this was God's doing. How grateful and happy it made me to feel that I had brought some comfort and hope to those dear people.

Victoria Booth Demarest — in 1975 — Still writing books, composing hymns, and preaching!

—Photo by Eleanor Lehner

A Sacred Arts International Photograph

In closing, I would like to witness to answered prayer.

When I was five years old, my mother had to leave for a great campaign in Rouen, France. She told me later that I pleaded, "Ne pars pas, Maman. Reste avec nous." (Don't leave, Mother. Stay with us.) My tearful face at the window, she said, would haunt her for days and nights. But my sister, Evangeline, who had just turned six, asked, "Maman, if you go to Rouen, will souls be saved that would not be saved if you did not go?" "Yes, Darling." "Then go, Maman."

A lady professor in Rouen wrote a letter to my mother expressing deep gratitude for the change in her soul resulting from their encounter. She added, "Be blessed in your children; I hope they will one day reward you nobly for all your sacrifices." And in a letter to a friend from Le Havre, where she had one of the most terrible battles at the beginning and one of the greatest victories at the end of her campaign, my mother wrote: "Do you know what the 'Centuple' [the 'hundredfold' promised by Jesus] is for me? That my children shall become apostles! *I claim this from God, and, do you know, there is an assurance in my heart!*" Her own mother, Catherine Booth, as she lay dying, said to her children, who were gathered around her bed: "I gave you all to God before I had any of you or any prospect of you... I said, 'God, they shall be Thine *down to the third and fourth generation.*'"

Both my grandmother's and my mother's prayers were answered in my becoming an apostle of Jesus Christ. And even more was granted, for I have before me a letter from the fifth generation, my granddaughter, Mary Sutton Monro McGregor (daughter of my eldest daughter, Mrs. Claxton Monro). I quote:

> Ever since I was a little girl I've been very proud of my Grandmother because of her extensive ministry to all people. I have been inspired by your dynamic and relevant preaching. You always were able to surprise a congregation into paying careful attention to what you had to say, despite the prejudice against women ministers by the average person. Your spiritual strength and dedication to the Lord inspires me to seek his help in living a life that is meaningful.

Yes, "they shall be Thine down to the third and fourth generation." And, I add, the fifth.

Chapter Eight

THE CHALLENGE OF TODAY

A MULTITUDE OF PROBLEMS

Christianity today is being challenged as never before — challenged by communism — by spiritual ignorance — by world hunger — by racial injustice — by competing religions and by what sometimes seem to be almost overwhelming evidences of universal inhumanity.

At the same time our nation faces an assortment of dilemmas that man is obviously incapable of solving on his own. These include the problems of drug and alcohol abuse, high suicide rate, race struggles, violence, and crime. Added to these are feelings of individual insignificance and powerlessness in a mass society, cynicism about governmental operations, and despair aroused by the ravaging of natural resources.

Personal morality has bogged down in a permissive, material-oriented society, in which Christian principles are ridiculed and the power of prayer has been forgotten.

The media keeps us posted on such evils as cheating in colleges and universities, unrestricted sex indulgence, casual abortion, child abuse and neglect. Teenagers and even little children are becoming alcoholics. Statistics reveal the increasingly high percentage of divorces. Assassinations and attempted assassinations occur with alarming frequency. Kidnappings proliferate. Bombs explode in improbable places. Crime attains appalling proportions. Life is endangered not only on the highways but even in the seclusion of the home. Policemen are shot in their own homes just because they are policemen. Our families are breaking up. It is needless to go on.

"Men loved darkness rather than light,"° Jesus told Nicodemus. "This is the condemnation." More than any other nation, America was blessed with light. The early settlers came to this country because they wanted freedom to follow that "light." But light has been turned into darkness — blessings into temptations, tolerance into indulgence, discipline into permissiveness, temperance into drunkenness, freedom into licentiousness and anarchy.

Spiritual retrogression in America began when faith in science and technology was substituted for faith in God. The resulting disillusionment has only increased our problems. It is as though our society is being ravaged by an epidemic of spiritual deficiency in which every available spiritual doctor is needed. The prophecy of Amos is being fulfilled.[1] There is a worldwide famine for the word of God.

Our nation needs to hear the words, "Thus saith the Lord," spoken from every pulpit. And just as they were *at the birth of Christianity — witness Mary, Elizabeth, and Anna — they must be spoken by women as well as by men.*

"At the birth of Christianity!" If it is to meet the challenge of today it is evident that Christianity itself needs a new birth. Even leaders in certain churches and theological schools have lost vision and faith. A shocking number of theological students have admitted that they have no devotional life.[2] And everywhere the Christian image has been tarnished by the wide discrepancy between the *standards* and the *behavior* of those who profess Christianity.

A RETURN TO BASICS

Distressed by the sad condition of the Anglican Church in England, the Archbishop of Canterbury, Donald Coggan, called for a "return to basics." "Each man and woman matters," he wrote. "The family matters, good work matters, the other fellow matters."[3]

"A return to basics." The greatest basic to which Christianity must return for a rebirth can be stated in one word, LOVE. In the Scriptures we do not read, "God is power," or "God is wisdom." Nor is he given the name of any of his attributes save one. "GOD IS LOVE,"[4] said John the apostle. And that love encompasses every other single attribute, even as the white light of the sun contains every color of the rainbow.

Christianity needs to experience a new baptism of love for God and for man. As a little girl of five, I preached my first "sermon" — so said my nurse. I was playing in a park in Paris when suddenly I saw a man, dirty and in rags, sitting on a bench with his head in his hands. His tears were falling to the ground. I ran to him, bent my head so that I could look into his face, and said, "Ne pleure pas. Dieu t'aime, et moi je t'aime aussi." (Don't cry. God loves you and I love you, too!) The man smiled.

To say, "God loves you," is not enough. We only mock man's needs unless we can add, "and I love you too," and *demonstrate it.* And to say, "I love you," is also not enough. Human love is not sufficient to heal the wounds of human souls. That is why social work alone falls short. Jesus said, "Man shall not (indeed cannot) live by bread alone."[5] Man needs to experience the healing and renewing grace of the love of God — that experience which changes sinners into saints.

Six verses of Scripture give us the "basics" of Christianity.

"God is *love."*[4]

"God so *loved* the world that He gave His only begotten Son — that whosoever believeth on Him should not perish but have everlasting life."[6]

"Thou shalt *love* the Lord thy God with all thy

heart and with all thy soul and with all thy mind and with all thy strength, this is the first commandment, and the second is like unto it, Thou shalt *love* thy neighbor as thyself."[7]

"By *this* (not by your profession) shall all men *know* that you are my disciples, by your *love* one to another."[8]

"*Love* your enemies, bless those that curse you, do good to those who despitefully use you, so shall you be the children of your Father, which is in Heaven."[9]

"*Love* is the fulfillment of the law."[10]

These verses are bound together by the one word, LOVE. No wonder St. Augustine said to his monks, "Love, love, love, then do as you like."

Without love, the gift of faith, of miracles, of prophetic preaching or any other gift of the Spirit, is "nothing."[11]

Without love, the ministry is barren. Without love, religion — even the Christian religion — becomes a Void, a Mockery, a Monster.

Religion without the love of God as revealed in Christ is the sheep seeking the shepherd. True Christianity is the shepherd seeking and finding the lost sheep. The father running to meet his repentant prodigal son. God coming down to man in the body and blood of Christ. Men and women proclaiming that love and *demonstrating it by their deeds.*

THE MOTHER INSTINCT

God's ministry is a ministry of love. And woman is peculiarly fitted for that ministry. Even more than man, she is qualified to calm those who are troubled and to comfort those who suffer. Who better than she can understand the meaning of the Cross? Does she not risk death to bring forth new life?

Woman's spiritual ministry is the extension of the mother-instinct, adding to this beautiful quality the power, wisdom, and divine love given by the Holy Spirit.

When consecrated and extended to the service of humanity, the mother-instinct becomes a powerful asset. Bible and church history reveal women who were great saints because they were great mothers and great mothers because they were great saints. Mary, the mother of Jesus, Monica, the mother of St. Augustine, Susanna Wesley, Catherine Booth. And many, many more. Most of the Quaker, Methodist, and Salvation Army women ministers were also wives and mothers. Other women who remained single, in every denomination, especially Roman Catholic saints, consecrated their mother-instinct and became spiritual mothers of thousands. Never was spiritual motherhood more needed than today.

Jesus said, "Peter, do you love me?" and upon receiving an affirmative answer, he commanded, "Feed my sheep."[12] Dare anyone say that this command was given only to men?

What difference does it make whether the hands that break the sacramental bread at the altar are feminine or masculine hands, or whether the divine food in prophetic preaching or in pastoral ministration is given by a man or a woman minister? *The important thing is that the people be fed.* The manner in which they are fed, the place and the sex of the minister, these things are inconsequential.

"A return to basics." Jesus challenged his disciples to attend to basics. He said, "Why call ye me Lord, Lord, and *do not* the things that I say?"[13] His words ring in our ears. "Depart from me, you cursed . . . for I was hungry and you gave me no food . . . thirsty and you gave me no drink . . . naked and you did not clothe me. . . ."[14] To

God, Woman, & Ministry

P. 95 — Royden —
15t woman to
occupy Calvin's
pulpit.

P. 99 — Episcopal priest —
scratched female
priest's hand as he
received Communion.

P. 110 —
15t sermon — 6

P. 135 Offered ordination
2 X — didn't want to
be exception

P. 137 — Presbyterian
General Ass. turned
down Overture d
on Ordination Of
women.

P. 151 — Women deprived
of official recognition
by church — pastors
or priests in all
but name?

Jim P.151 Wallis. —

Distorted Exegesis —
subordinates women.

P.151 — What authority
can any Church refuse
Ordination — those
whose ministry God
has honored.

P.152 — Women's message
Thus saith the Lord.

P.155 —
Prophet voice —
has no sex —
Samuel — Called
by God — to warn Eli.

P.157 C.S. Lewis —
man may not represent
God to the people.

P.159
Body of Christ —
Minister ministers — to
Whole Body — Catherine
Booth — Mother Seton

those who asked when they had left such things undone, he replied, "Anything you did not do for one of these, however humble, you did not do for me."[15]

When women ministers are rejected by the church, much is left undone for the Lord.

"WHATSOEVER THINGS ARE JUST" [16]

Is it right for women to be deprived of official recognition by the church when they are pastors or priests *in all but name?* (So often the case on mission fields and in evangelistic work.) God does not discriminate between his children. Should the church do so?

To turn aside the proffered services of competent, spirit-filled ministers simply because they are female rather than male, would seem to dishonor the church more than it dishonors the women rejected. It is comparable to withholding medical aid from those who are suffering or even dying.

Post American editor, Jim Wallis, is quoted as saying, "The church must face up to the issue of Equal Rights for women or it will lose the most sensitive young women it now has. *Distorted exegesis must no longer be used by men to support a status quo that subordinates women.*"[17] And "I am appalled," writes Richard Pierard, Indiana State University professor of history, "at the large number of books and articles that continue to pour from evangelical presses propagating this outdated concept (the subordination of women.)" He adds that the church needs to "challenge and refute the sexist doctrines so latent in our faith as practiced today."[18]

We must ask, by what authority can any church refuse ordination to those whose ministry God has honored? Is the church greater than God? Is it not an insult to the Holy Spirit to introduce the question of sex, a physical accident, into His rights and privileges? When a woman is truly the mouthpiece of the Holy Spirit she is not conscious of her sex . . . and *neither are her hearers.* Her message is, "Thus saith the Lord."

The church throughout the world has suffered and is still suffering incalculable loss by having refused, and in many cases still refusing, to confirm an ordination given by the Holy Spirit to women equipped and prepared for the ministry.

A rebirth of Christianity today will include the recognition by the church of woman's rights to the ordained ministry. When justice speaks, man's ideal nature, made in God's image, deplores discrimination. We are offered a choice between the power of light or the power of darkness — between the loving will of God or the selfish whim of man.

WHAT IS THE CHURCH?

Just what is the church, we might pause to ask?

First let us consider what the church is NOT. The church is not a building, humble or magnificent. It is not an institution — Presbyterian, Episcopal, Baptist, Methodist, Roman Catholic, or what you will. It is not a man-made organization.

The church is a living organism, born of the Holy Spirit on the Day of Pentecost. It is the company of men and women, all over the world, *in whom the spirit of Christ dwells.*[19]

In the New Testament the church is described as being: "A Temple" — built of "living stones."[20]

"A Body" — the mystical body of Christ.[21]

"A Bride" — the bride of Christ.[22]

And Christ has only one Temple — not two or two hundred. He has only one Body. He has only one Bride. (No divorce there.)

Just as every follower of Christ as Lord and Savior, of whatever church affiliation, age, sex, nation, race, or occupation, black or white, plumber or president, waitress or archbishop, is a living stone in that Temple, so is he or she a member of the mystical Body of Christ.

And just as a deep sleep fell on the first Adam and out of his side was taken his bride, Eve, so the deep sleep of death fell on the second Adam, Christ; and his side was pierced; and blood and water flowed from out his heart.[23] And from that heart was born the church — his Bride. He gave his life for her. He gave his life to her. Every born-again Christian whether man or woman, symbolically represents that Bride.

There is only one Church. There has never been but one Church from the Day of Pentecost. There will never be *more than one Church.*[24] *The real Church of Christ can-cannot be controlled by man.*

Christians should joyfully accept the fact that, regardless of the variety of beliefs and forms of worship in its many denominations, even regardless of some errors in doctrine in some of its branches, *the One Church Is.*

This oneness of the church was brought home to me when, preaching throughout Europe, I partook of the same sacrament whether kneeling at the altar with Episcopalians, or served by the Waldensian elders around the Lord's table, or seated in the pews of Methodist or Presbyterian churches. I realized more than ever that all true Christians, no matter their sex or their diversity in language, dress, or customs, are united and represented in the body and blood of our Lord. They are ONE in their love and allegiance to him and it is a joyous and glorious union.

From time to time reformations have been needed

to purify the organized church. And throughout church history new denominations and Christian movements have come into being. *They have all made important contributions to the ONE CHURCH* — either when certain Christian truths and doctrines, otherwise forgotten, denied or neglected, needed to be revived, preached, and practiced; or when new methods for reaching the indifferent needed to be improvised (re: the Salvation Army). The charismatic movement now sweeping the Christian world is a new example. Although it may overstress the importance of "speaking in tongues," it serves a useful function by emphasizing the actuality of the Holy Spirit as a power for meeting the spiritual needs of contemporary churches.

The church as a whole meets humanity's need for a variety of forms in which to worship. Some people want to pray with shouts of "Hallelujah!" . . . with music . . . with dancing. Others prefer to worship while immersed in the silent music of the stars — too distant for human ears.

Let us thank God for the visible church, no matter its name, which gives us divine protection and nurture from our birth to our death.

> *Oh Church of Christ, men need thy lights*
> *clear shining*
> *Mid city streets and quiet country ways;*
> *For babel sounds and transient gleams ill-guiding,*
> *Have drawn their feet within a wild'ring maze. . .*
>
> —Effie Hussey[25]

THE MEANING OF CHURCH MINISTERING

It is also essential for Christians to understand the various ministries of the church. These are 1) the Prophetic, 2) the Pastoral; 3) the Sacramental; and, we may add, 4) the Healing.

The title "Minister" or "Priest" does not limit the function. Some ministers or priests are mainly prophets. Others are mainly pastors. Only a few excel as both. That is why lay ministries are needed to supply whatever may be lacking.

Jesus spoke of himself as being preeminently our *Savior*.[26] Nevertheless, as a minister, he was prophet, pastor, and healer. And in the Epistle to the Hebrews, he is referred to as "our great High Priest."[27] As a prophet he proclaimed and exemplified the relationship of God to humanity. As a pastor he gave personal attention to individuals, wherever he found them — beside a well, on the roadside, on a rooftop — ministering to whatever their needs might be. And he healed the multitudes.

And Jesus said: "As my Father sent me, so send I you."[28]

Without question, women prophets and pastors, apostles and ministers, missionaries and evangelists, have taken these words *to themselves* and have found in them strength and inspiration.

A prophet is a "voice,"[29] and a *"voice" has no sex.* A prophet may be a man, woman, or child. Witness the child Samuel, who, in the middle of the night, was called by God to warn Eli, the old priest, that judgment was coming upon him, because he had permitted his wicked sons to minister in the temple.[30] This illustrates the priority of the prophetic ministry, which informs and directs the other ministries of the Church.

THE PEOPLE'S NEEDS

In these times of crisis and revolution, women as well as men prophets are sorely needed, that they might rebuke evil, whether in church, nation, or world ... that they might unveil corruption, insist on justice, preach the will of God as revealed in the Scriptures, and, most importantly, the love of God revealed in Christ. Women can preach this love as well as men . . . sometimes even better than men. And preach it they should.

Equally needed in times of crisis are the pastoral services of a minister or priest, whether masculine or feminine, who is specially qualified to comfort, strengthen, and counsel the individual members of his/her own congregation when problems or tragedies beset them. Too often the fellowship, the prayers, the desperately needed spiritual assistance are nowhere to be found when trauma strikes.

If people could receive the personal pastoral help to which they are entitled, there would not be such a rush for the psychiatrist's couch. In this connection, it should be noted that men and women ministers should endeavor to become knowledgeable psychologists in order to deal adequately with the personal and spiritual needs of their parishioners.

The reverse is also true. A prominent woman professor of psychology and psychiatry, who was converted in one of my meetings, commented to me: "Before my conversion I could diagnose my patients' troubles and help them to understand themselves, but I had no *remedy* to offer. Now I can offer Christ as the great Healer."

Just think of it! A prominent psychologist — a woman — offering Christ to her patients. But if such a woman decided to become a minister there are those who would do everything in their power to stop her!

Is it not presumptuous for anyone to endeavor to dictate the manner in which God may use a person?

In the *New York Times* of September 17, 1976, Canon Allan Wendt, a black delegate to the Episcopal Convention, was quoted as saying that it would certainly be "ironic" if blacks joined forces with those who would keep women "spiritually and emotionally enslaved."

Christian history, including the experiences of thousands of women ministers, preachers, and evangelists, both inside and outside of the churches, causes me to cry out in indignant protest against such remarks as C. S. Lewis' dictum that a woman may properly represent the people to God but not God to the people,[31] which suggests that a woman might become a pastor but never a prophet! My whole life's ministry, which has been prophetic, has exemplified the very opposite. I was called and particularly qualified for the function of prophetic preaching. Other women may be called and especially qualified in various other areas.

Some, for example, may be called to minister to children. The inadequacy of a vast number of lay Sunday school teachers is tragic. Too many are satisfied to tell Bible stories without explaining how the deep spiritual significance of these stories can apply to the lives of the children in their classes. As the children grow older, therefore, they dismiss these stories along with fairy tales. Many children whose spiritual needs have been neglected drift into juvenile crime. Where are the ministers who could be solving this problem? Are they among the candidates for ordination who have been rejected because they are not men?

Replenishing the spiritual deficiency of our young people is another area in which women ministers could serve. Yet many churches today are being closed for lack of ministers, while the women who could fill their pulpits are shunted aside. If American citizens are not to be denied the spiritual guidance they need, multiple church ministries by both sexes are imperative.

However, since the spiritual condition of our people, which is poor, controls their economic priorities, we find ourselves in a sad situation. The decreasing number of salaried positions available is forcing candidates for the ministry into secular jobs. In view of the disastrous spiritual and moral situation in our country, it would seem that the salvation of our people should be considered a necessity rather than a luxury.

GOD'S INTENTIONS

I have always been impressed by the text: "My thoughts are not your thoughts, neither are your ways my ways."[32] To quote William Cowper's famous hymn: "God moves in a mysterious way, his wonders to perform."

Confining the activities of God's Spirit, in any sphere, to a single sex means that we pull him down to the level of our limited human knowledge and understanding. We diminish him. We dishonor him.

To fight the Spirit of God in a woman is to fight God himself. God is not divided against himself. The spirit of God in a male minister would not fight the Spirit of God in a female minister. The spirit of envy perhaps. The spirit of pride. The fear of competition. But never the Spirit of God.

It is interesting to note that the disciples of Jesus are given only one male appellation in the New Testament. Jesus called them "Brother."[33] In fact, he *forbade* that they be called "Father."[34] On the other hand, disciples are given three female appellations. Jesus called them "Sister" and "Mother,"[35] and in the Gospel of John and in the Book of Revelation (together with men disciples), they are called "Bride."[36] By what logic can disciples called "Sister," "Mother," or "Bride" of Christ be forbidden to function as his ministers — the ministers of His Church?

The principal of sexism when applied to the ministry could be interpreted as follows:

Honor the man minister because he is a man — even

though he may be totally ineffective as a minister.

Reject the woman because she is a woman, even though she may be well qualified as a minister and filled with the spirit of God.

This attitude would be a flagrant denial of the God-intended democratic nature of the church.

The Woman's Declaration of Independence, adopted at the Seneca Falls Convention, July 19-20, 1848, offers an interesting commentary. (See Appendix G)

THE CHURCH — A DEMOCRACY

In the beginning the church was the greatest example of democratic organization ever given to humanity.

Witness the following words of St. Paul, founder of Christian churches. Regarding the body of Christ, the church, he wrote:

> *The eye cannot say to the hand, I have no need of you, neither can the head say to the feet, I have no need of you . . . every member ministers to the whole body. If one member is honored all the members rejoice with it.*[37]

As mother of the Salvation Army, Catherine Booth ministered to the whole body of Christ throughout the world. So did Maude Royden as ordained minister of the City Temple in London. So did the recently sainted Mother Seton (Elizabeth Ann), an Episcopalian, a devoted wife and mother, and a beautiful Christian character, who, after she became a Roman Catholic nun, founded the "first religious order of women in America, the Sisters of Charity, in 1808. It now has 8,000 sisters in six communities on three continents."[38] Countless other great women have ministered in their own individual ways.

According to the apostle Paul, every member of the

body of Christ should rejoice in the honors bestowed upon these women. And, rather than discourage women from entering the ministry, every member of the Body of Christ should pray that *God may raise others like them* in this day of great spiritual need.

It is also true to the democratic ideal of the church that every group of people in its membership, no matter their race, class, or sex, should be represented in its decisions and activities.

"How can I be 'advisor on women's affairs' when my church does not grant women even minor orders or a voice and vote in any key decision-making body?" said Sister Margaret Ellen Traxler, founder of the Roman Catholic National Coalition of American Nuns, when she declined an invitation to serve as advisor to the World Council of Churches Fifth General Assembly, held in Nairobi, Kenya, in 1975. "I believe that continued discrimination against women by organized religion will empty our churches," she added, "because younger women will not abide any church that denies them fullness of rights and presence within a-worshipping body."

No doubt it takes time for a society to move from institutionalized male chauvinism to the full recognition of woman's equality. But again, in all honesty, we must admit that the Holy Spirit expressed that recognition, through the lips of the apostle Peter, on the birthday of the church — the Day of Pentecost.[40]

Why should woman wait so long for man to comply? Today, the world has accepted this principle in almost every other area. How can the church, which was given the opportunity to set an example so many centuries ago, still tolerate its own inconsistencies?

Is the authority of the church hierarchy greater than that of the Holy Spirit, the leader of the church — *without whom the church would not exist; without whom it becomes completely ineffectual?*

"It is sad," a lawyer recently remarked to me, "that the church which logically should be leader in matters that concern human happiness, is so often the follower."

Let me illustrate: Women have entered industry, business, all the professions, the sports, the arts, even government on an equal basis with men. We even have women in the military academies. Women are officers in the Army and Navy. Why should women be trained and commissioned to kill and not trained and ordained to save?

In the 1975 special issue of the *Inter-Dependent,* page 125, the United Nations, in its Declaration on the Elimination of Discrimination, states that "The full and complete development of a country, the welfare of the world and the cause of peace requires the maximum participation of women as well as men *in all fields,"* and that *"women should be included in policy-making and program-planning positions."* This from the United Nations.

By contrast, Eldom Tanner, the Mormon first counselor, in opposing the Equal Rights Amendment, wrote, "God has clearly defined woman's position, duties and destiny . . . one of woman's greatest privileges, blessings and opportunities is to be a co-partner with God in bringing his children (meaning babies) into the world."

What about being a partner with God in bringing his *spiritual* children into the world!

SIGNS OF PROGRESS

When Antoinette Brown entered the Oberlin Theological Seminary in 1847, her father wrote to her: "I am shocked by your audacity and lack of wisdom."[42] In 1853 she became the first ordained woman minister in the United States.

In 1868, the Reverend Phoebe Hanaford compiled a list of ninety-seven prominent American women. Fifty-seven of them were preachers!

In 1976, 108 years later, the Reverend Evelyn Newman was installed as the first woman minister of the Riverside Church in New York City. At the time, the Reverend Dr. Ernest T. Campbell, senior minister, commented, "That she is a woman is secondary to the fact that she is a human being who is vitally in touch with the love of God. Were she to merely live among us would be gain. That she will work among us too calls for thanks to God."[43]

It is evident that the church throughout the world has made great strides forward in the matter of woman's ministry. Throughout Europe and in Asia and Africa, women are now being ordained by most Protestant churches. Even in the Roman Catholic church there is a revolution, triggered by the encyclical "Pacem in Terris" of Pope John XXIII. Thousands of nuns have left the seclusion of their convents in order to minister more effectively in every sphere of human life. Father Kung, a prominent Roman Catholic theologian in Holland, states that there are no theological reasons for excluding women from the priesthood. An eighteen-year-old girl preaches at a Roman Catholic Mass in South America. The Queen of England receives Communion from the hands of a woman elder in a church in Scotland, Anglican bishops in England, Jamaica, and New Zealand have approved the ordination of women priests, Anglican bishops in Canada have adopted it. And on September 16, 1976, the Episcopal Church of America agreed to ordain women.

Women are flocking to the seminaries of every Christian denomination. Woman's rights to be ordained by all Christian churches should no longer be questioned or denied.

What God has to say to the church NOW is supremely important. NOT yesterday. Not tomorrow. NOW.

"I am convinced," says Alexander Solzhenitsyn, "that the only salvation for the East and also for the West, which is also in a dangerous situation, lies in a moral and religious rebirth."[44]

TO MEET THE CHALLENGE

We need another "Great Awakening" like that which led to the birth of the nation.

"The date we should be celebrating is not the organizational birth of the nation in 1776, but its organic birth in 1740," said noted church historian, Winthrop Hudson.[45] "It was 'the Great Awakening,' not the trigger issue of taxation which transformed the colonial consciousness to create the American identity.

> The Awakening played an important role in forming a national consciousness among people of different colonies whose primary ties were with Europe rather than with one another. As a spontaneous movement which swept across all colonial boundaries, generated a common interest and a common loyalty, bound people together in a common cause and reinforced *the common conviction that God has a special destiny for America,* the Awakening contributed greatly to the development of a sense of cohesiveness among American people.

A *Rebirth of Christianity* in America would inevitably lead to a national spiritual renewal — a spiritual Great Awakening.

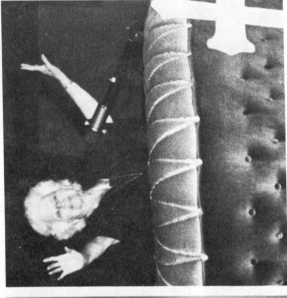

Victoria Booth Demarest

Conducting a Preaching Mission
Queensway Cathedral
Toronto, Ontario, November, 1976

Reading her play *My Son Jesus*
First Methodist Church, St. Petersburg,
Florida Chain of Missions, 1954

–Photo by Gábor Eder   *Sacred Arts International Photographs*

There is another America besides the one of which I gave such a dark picture in the beginning of this chapter — an America which I love, brave, strong, and hopeful. There is much evidence that the Spirit of God is working in this America. We can sense a new awareness of the theological facts of sin, judgment and forgiveness. We believe America is in the throes of spiritual gestation.

To be a minister of Christ is the highest honor that can be conferred. The privilege of turning men and women from darkness to light, of contributing to the salvation of souls, of expanding the church, of strengthening the kingdom of God on earth — what could be a greater vocation? Anyone, man or woman, who has heard the divine call to devote his or her life to this highest of all causes should do so only in the spirit of deepest humility — mingled with courage, faith, determination, and utmost consecration — recognizing his or her utter dependence upon God. Only in this spirit can anyone succeed.

In closing I would say to young women who plan to enter the ministry:

Be certain that your motivation is right. In other words, that you are not entering the ministry for a career, because of women's lib or for any reason other than a truly divine call.

Choose a seminary where you not only get the necessary scholarly preparation but where your spiritual life and faith will be strengthened and not diminished (tragically the case in some instances).

Be of good courage. Do not let seemingly insurmountable difficulties daunt you. Remember the words of Jesus that if we have faith even as a grain of mustard seed we may command mountains to be cast into the sea and it shall be done.[46]

For a woman to be a true minister of Christ these days calls for heroism. But we are told to be good soldiers of Jesus Christ, and he has provided the armor.[47] "Fight the good fight of faith" and you, too, will have the joy of turning men from darkness to light and from the power of Satan to the power of God.[48]

Oh God, send a spiritual renewal to America. . .

that little children may be taught to listen to and heed your voice in their hearts,

that young people may be satisfied in their search for truth and goodness,

that husbands and wives may be reconciled and their love deepened and purified by your love,

that working men and women may be guided by you in finding solutions for their problems,

that those in business and the professions may seek the good of others rather than their own,

that those in government may rely on the wisdom you have promised in directing the affairs of men and nations,

that those in the ministry may preach your truth and your word, not their own ideas, and thus feed the people,

that American Christians may lead the Christians of the world in feeding starving millions of men, women, and children. . . .

Oh God, send a spiritual renewal to America. . . .

And grant that women may play their rightful part!

APPENDICES

APPENDIX A

Since William Booth's daughters were widely known before marriage under their maiden names, he had his sons-in-law legally attach the name *Booth* to their own surnames. Hence the names became:

Catherine Booth-Clibborn, born September 18, 1858. Founder of the Salvation Army in France, Switzerland, Holland and Belgium. See *The Maréchale*, by James Strachan (Hodder and Stoughton, Ltd., New York, 1914. Several editions, the last by Bethany Fellowship). On February 8, 1887, she married Arthur Sidney Clibborn, of distinguished Quaker descent, her chief of staff.

Emma Moss Booth-Tucker, born January 8, 1860. Founder with her husband, Frederick St. George de Lautour Tucker, of the Salvation Army in India. In 1896 she succeeded her brother, Ballington Booth, as Commander of the Salvation Army in the United States when the latter resigned and founded, with his wife Maude (nee Charlesworth), the Volunteers of America. See *Soldiers Without Swords*, by Herbert A. Wisbey, Jr. (The Macmillan Company, New York, 1955). Maude, called "Little Mother" by convicts whom she helped, became famous for prison reform work. See *Look Up and Hope*, by Susan F. Welty (Thomas Nelson and Sons, New York, 1961).

Evangeline Booth, born December 25, 1865, became Commander of the Salvation Army in the United States after Emma was killed in 1903 in a railroad accident. In 1934 she became the third *Booth* General of the Salvation Army. (The second was her eldest brother, Bramwell.) See *General*

Evangeline Booth by P. W. Wilson (Charles Scribner's Sons, New York, 1948), also *Soldiers Without Swords*, Op. Cit.

Lucy Booth-Hellberg, born April 28, 1867. Founder with her husband, Emmanuel Daniel Booth-Hellberg, of the Salvation Army in Scandinavia. See *Soldiers Without Swords*, Op. Cit.

APPENDIX B

I should like to provide a few facts to clarify the confusion regarding my maternal ancestry.

General William Booth, born 1829, died 1912.

Catherine Mumford Booth, born 1829, died 1890.

Order of the Booth children:

William Bramwell, born 1856, Second General of the Salvation Army following his father's death.

Ballington, born 1857. Commanded Salvation Army in the United States. Withdrew in 1896. Founded Volunteers of America.

Catherine, "La Maréchale," born 1858. Founded Salvation Army in France, Switzerland, Holland, and Belgium.

Emma Moss, born 1860. Founded Salvation Army in India.

Herbert, born 1862. Founded Salvation Army in Australia and New Zealand. Commanded Salvation Army in the United States.

Marian, born 1864. An invalid.

Eva (Evangeline), born 1865. Commanded Salvation Army in the United States. Elected Third Booth General of Salvation Army in 1934.

Lucy Milward, born 1867. Founded Salvation Army in Scandinavia.

William and Catherine Booth lie side by side in the

Salvation Army Cemetery in Abney Park, London. A memorial to William Booth in Westminster Abbey was dedicated in 1965, the Centennial of the founding of the Salvation Army.

The organization of the Salvation Army was patterned after that of a military army, and its General had absolute authority over its worldwide forces. The "orders and regulations" of the "International Headquarters" in London were enforced on the organization in every country where it was in operation.

Catherine Booth-Clibborn, the eldest daughter, was the first to found the organization outside of England. Commissioned by her father in 1881 to carry the Army to France, she sought to adapt it to the French culture and temperament. (Later she carried it to Switzerland, Holland and Belgium.)

Ballington Booth, the second son, sought to do the same for America when he was appointed commander in the United States. As a naturalized American, he disagreed with his father about the British, authoritarian character of the Army.

This caused conflict with William Booth and with International Headquarters and ultimately resulted in the first resignation of a Booth from the Salvation Army, 1896. Ballington and his wife Maude then founded the Volunteers of America.

A similar conflict between William Booth, International Headquarters, and my parents as well as doctrinal differences between my father, the gentle *Quaker,* and William Booth, the *Commanding General,* finally compelled my parents, at that time in Holland, to resign from the Army in January of 1902. (I was twelve years old then.) My parents gave themselves to world evangelism.

The similar conflict also compelled another son of William Booth, Herbert, commander in Australia, to resign in May of 1902.

William Booth believed in changing the sphere of command of his officers every several years and did not make an exception of his children. It broke my mother's heart when he removed her from France in 1896 and ordered her to Holland.

The second General of the Salvation Army, Bramwell Booth, continued the system of Government established by his father. But in 1922 when he ordered the transfer of his sister Evangeline Booth away from the command of the United States forces, she rebelled.

At her instigation, the High Council of all national commanders was called in London. The law which provided that each General would appoint his or her successor, was changed to making the office of General elective. Two non-Booth Generals were elected in succession (Generals Higgins and Osborne). Then Evangeline Booth was elected General of the whole Salvation Army in 1934.

APPENDIX C

Before I was fifteen years of age God had, in an especial manner, taught me what I consider the first and fundamental and all-comprehensive principle of Christ's salvation, of real Christianity — that every act of our lives, every relationship into which we enter, every object at which we aim, every purpose that inspires our souls, should be centered and bounded by God and His glory. I had embraced that idea of Christianity so early, and I can say before God and my own conscience that I sought to carry out that principle.

—*Catherine Booth*

W. T. Stead, *Life of Mrs. Booth* (Fleming H. Revell Co., 1900) p. 44-50.

APPENDIX D

Professor Harnack's hypothesis was published in January, 1900, on pages 16-41 of the *Zeitschrift für die Neutestamentlishe Wissenschaft* in an article entitled "The Probability of the Address and the Author of the Letter to the Hebrews." In a personal letter to Dr. Lee Anna Starr he subsequently summarized his conclusions as follows:

1. We can undoubtedly be assured that the letter was written to Rome — not to the church, but to the inner circle. Romans 15:5.

2. It is an amazing fact that the name of the author is lost. All names mentioned as possible authors do not explain why the earliest tradition blotted it out.

3. The problem is this: Since the letter (according to the closing verses of Chapter 13) was written by a person of high standing and an apostolic teacher of equal rank with Timothy, — if Luke, or Clemens, or Barnabas, or Apollos, had written it, we do not understand why their names or signatures should have been obliterated, hence we must look for a person who was intimately associated with Paul and Timothy, as the author, that we may understand why the name is not given. This can only be Priscilla:

(a) She had so-called inner circle in Rome — "The church that is in their house" (Romans 16:5).

(b) She was an Apostolic teacher of high standing, and known throughout Christendom of that day (Romans chapter 16).

(c) She was the teacher of the intelligent and highly educated Apollos (Acts 18).

(d) She and Aquila labored and taught together, and thus we see "I," and then again the pronoun "we" used.

APPENDIX E

In the Epistle to the Hebrews itself, we find criteria to aid us in our search for the author.

1. — Its writer was undoubtedly a Jew;
2. — A Hellenist;
3. — A nonresident of Palestine;
4. — Unacquainted with the details of the Temple ritual;
5. — Wrote;
6. — The disciple of an Apostle;
7. — A friend of Timothy;
8. — Had personal acquaintance with the addressed;
9. — Well-versed in Old Testament Scripture;
10. — Had access to Alexandrian Jewish literature, and knowledge of the teachings of Philo;
11. — Within the Pauline circle, and attached to Pauline theology;
12. — A scholar of marked ability and attainment;
13. — An individual of prominence and of authority in the primitive church.

Dr. Lee Anna Starr, *The Bible Status of Woman*, p. 190. (Fleming H. Revell Co., N.Y., 1926.)

APPENDIX F

The Clibborn lineage is traceable to the following seven barons: William de Lanvallei, Richard de Clare, Gilbert de Clare, Robert de Vere, Faire de Quincey, Roger Bigod, and Hugh Bigod.

The remaining barons were William Mowbray, Richard Montfichet, Roger Montgegon, William de Albini, Hanry Bohun, John Fitzrobert, Robert Fitzwalter, William de Fortibus, William de Hardell, William de Huntington, John de Lacie, William Malet, Jeffrey de Mandebille, and William Marshall.

APPENDIX G

Woman's Declaration of Independence
(A Resolution adopted at Seneca Falls Convention,
July 19-20, 1848)

"That, being invested by the Creator with the same capabilities and the same consciousness of responsibility for their exercise, it is demonstrably the right and duty of woman, equally with man, to promote every righteous cause by every righteous means; and especially in regard to the great subjects of morals and religion it is self-evidently her right to participate with her brother in teaching them, both in private and by writing and by speaking, by any instrumentalities proper to be used, and in any assemblies proper to be held; and this being self-evident truth, growing out of the divinely implanted principles of human nature, any custom or authority adverse to it, whether modern or wearing the hoary sanction of antiquity, is to be regarded as a self-evident falsehood and at war with mankind."

[From *The Bible Status of Woman*, Lee Anna Starr, p. 416 (Fleming H. Revell Co., N.Y., 1926)]

REFERENCES

PREFACE

[1]The Rt. Rev. Daniel Corrigan; the Rt. Rev. Robert DeWitt; the Rt. Rev. Edward R. Welles II. (Italics by Victoria Booth Demarest.)

[2]Progress Report to the House of Bishops from the Committee to Study the Proper Place of Women in the Ministry of the Church, authorized by the House of Bishops in September, 1965. Members appointed by the Presiding Bishop: The Bishop of Rochester (The Rt. Rev. George W. Barrett), Chairman; Mrs. Irvin Bussing, California, Secretary; The Bishop of Oklahoma (The Rt. Rev. Chilton Powell); The Bishop of New Hampshire (The Rt. Rev. Charles F. Hall); Mrs. Charles M. Hawes III, the Virgin Islands; The Rev. Alden D. Kelley, Bexley Hall; Dr. Cynthia Wedel, Virginia (Italics by V.B.D.)

[3]See *The Life of Catherine Booth, Mother of the Salvation Army.* 2 vol. By Frederick de Lautour Booth-Tucker (Fleming H. Revell Co., 1892). Also *Catherine Booth* by Catherine Bramwell-Booth (Hodder and Stoughton, Ltd., London, 1970).

[4]The Rev. Maude Royden, *The Church and Woman* (James Clarke & Co., London; George H. Doran Co., New York, 1926).

[5]Dr. Katherine Bushnell, *God's Word to Women*, (Privately published, 1912). Available: Library of Congress, New York Public Library, Oakland Public Library, British Museum. 398 pages.

[6]Lee Anna Starr, D.D., LL.D., *The Bible Status of Women*, (Fleming H. Revell, New York, Chicago, London, Edinburgh, 1926).

[7]Luke 12:48 (KJV)

CHAPTER ONE

[1]John 4:24

[2]Genesis 1:27

[3]Genesis 1:1, Living Bible; Genesis 1:2, Amplified Bible

[4]Isaiah 66: 7-13

[5]*The Creation* by James Weldon Johnson (1871-1938). See A. Adoff, *The Poetry of Black America* (Harper & Row, 1973).

[6]Proverbs 9: 1-3

[7]Colossians 2:9

[8]Matthew 23:37; Luke 13:34

[9]John 14:16

[10]Luke 15: 8, 9

[11]Jeremiah 31:9 (as a father); Isaiah 66:9 (as a mother)

[12]Matthew 21:16

[13]Virginia Ramey Mollenkort, *Milton the Awakener*. (Christianity Today, 11/8/74)

[14]Nancy Hardesty, *Great Women of Faith*, (Eternity, 12/74) — Italics by V. B. Demarest.

[15]Mark Twain, *Joan of Arc* (Harper Brothers, N. Y., 1896)

[16]Galatians 5:22, 23

[17]Ephesians 6:11

[18]II Timothy 2:3

[19]Psalms 8:5

[20]Genesis 1:28

[21]Galatians 3:28
[22]W. T. Stead, *Life of Mrs. Booth*, Fleming & Revell, 1900.
[23]Adiel J. Moncrief, D.D., *Religion in Today's World*, October 30, 1976.

CHAPTER TWO

[1]Luke 1:30
[2]I. Corinthians 1:26-28
[3]Luke 1:38
[4]Luke 1:46-55
[5]Galatians 4:4
[6]Genesis 3:15
[7]Luke 2:49
[8]John 2:1-3
[9]John 2:4, New English Bible, (Inversion-Ford Assoc., N. Y. 1965)
[10]John 2:3-9
[11]Acts 1:13-15; Acts 2:4, 18
[12]Luke 2:28-38
[13]Matthew 9:13-15
[14]Luke 7:11-15, KJV, R.S.V., N.E.B.
[15]John 4:9
[16]"Except a man be born again, he cannot see the kingdom of God."
John 3:3
[17]John 4:26
[18]John 4:39-42 (Italics by VBD)
[19]John 8:3, NEB; 8:11, KJV
[20]Luke 7:36-48
[21]Luke 18:1-5
[22]Luke 11:31
[23]Matthew 15:22-28
[24]Mark 5:25-34
[25]Mark 12:41-44, RSV
[26]Luke 10:41-42
[27]John II, RSV
[28]Acts 2:36
[29]Matthew 26:1-16; Mark 14:1-11; John 12:208.
Scholars agree that it was Mary of Bethany who annointed Jesus and was commended by him, although there are slight discrepancies in the three Gospel versions.
[30]John 19:25-27
[31]John 20
[32]Mark 14:50:52; Luke 22:54.
Scholars agree that John was the young man who tried to follow but had to flee when the linen cloth he wore was seized by a guard.
[33]Luke 22:55-62
[34]Luke 23:28
[35]Matthew 27:19

[36] John 20:17, 18
[37] I Corinthians 15:1-4
[38] Mark 16:9-14
[39] Matthew 12:50

CHAPTER THREE

[1] Acts 1:4-8, 13-15; Acts 2:4
[2] Acts 2:16-18. (Italics by VBD)
[3] Acts 2:6
[4] Galatians 3:26
[5] John 1:18 and I John 4:12
[6] John 8:12 and John 9:5
[7] I Corinthians 13
[8] Romans 5:8
[9] Mark 16:15
[10] Booth-Tucker, *Life of C. B.*, Vol. I, p. 359-362
[11] IBID., p. 363
[12] Royden, *The Church and Women*, p. 113, 114
[13] W. T. Stead, *Life of Mrs. Booth*, (Fleming H. Revell Co., New York, 1900)
[14] Acts 21:8, 9
[15] Romans 16:1 (R.S.V., N.E.B., Phillips).
[16] Romans 16:7
[17] Acts 16:14, 15, 40
[18] Acts 12:12 and I Corinthians 1:11
[19] Acts 17:34
[20] II Timothy 1:5; (Italics by VBD)
[21] Philippians 4:2
[22] Romans 16:6-12
[23] Colossians 4:15: Revised Standard, Phillips Modern English, New English, Amplified, New Testament in Modern English.
[24] Dr. Lee Anna Starr, *The Bible Status of Women* (Fleming H. Revell, N. Y., 1926, p. 271, 272)
[25] Acts 9:36-40; Dr. J. Hastings, *The Greater Men and Women of the Bible*, (Scribners, N. Y., 1916. Vol. VI, p. 171-181).
[26] Acts 18; I Cor. 16:19; II Tim. 4:19; See also Starr, p. 187-206; 262; Hastings, Vol. VI, p. 269-277 and 289.
[27] Starr, p. 188.
[28] Romans 16:3, 4
[29] Starr, p. 203
[30] J. D. Douglas, Ed., *The New International Dictionary of the Christian Church*, (Zondervan, Grand Rapids, Mich. 1974)
[31] Galatians 4:7
[32] Luke 24:49
[33] II Timothy 1:7 (Italics by VBD)

CHAPTER FOUR

[1] I Corinthians 14:34

[2] I Corinthians 11:5 (Italics by VBD)

[3] I Corinthians 12:10, 14:22, *Good News for Modern Man* (American Bible Society)

[4] I Corinthians 14:3. Helen B. Montgomery, A.M., D.H.L., LI.D., *The New Testament in Modern English*, American Baptist Publication Society (Judson Press, Philadelphia, 1924)

[5] I Corinthians 12:10, Goodspeed

[6] I Corinthians 12:10, Phillips Modern English

[7] I Corinthians 14:35

[8] I Corinthians 14:34-40. Katherine Bushnell: See Ref. No. 5, Preface. Helen B. Montgomery, Op. Cit. (Italics by VBD)

[9] The Rev. Mrs. Antoinette Brown Blackwell was ordained 9/15/1853 by the Congregational Church, Butler, N. Y. Karen Stone, *'Times they are a-changing?'* (Geneva *Times.* Reprinted in Episcopalian, 1/75).

[10] I Timothy 2:12, Phillips

[11] Galatians 3:28

[12] Acts 26:20-23; Galatians 2:11-21

[13] Philemon 1:1-25

[14] Acts 17:26

[15] Starr, *The Bible Status of Women*, Op. Cit., p. 241

[16] I Corinthians 11:3

[17] Romans 12:4, 5

[18] I Corinthians 7:34

[19] Colossians 1:18

[20] I Timothy 2:12. See also 10 above.

[21] Romans 13:1-8

[22] II Corinthians 6:3

[23] Titus 2:3-8, N.E.B., Phillips

[24] Starr, op. cit., p. 271-272

[25] Starr, op. cit., p. 188, 202, 262

[26] C. Bramwell Booth, *Catherine Booth — The Story of Her Loves* (Hodder & Stoughton, London, 1970)

[27] II Corinthians 3:6

[28] Galatians 5:1

[29] I Corinthians 11:11 (New Testament in Modern English)

CHAPTER FIVE

[1] N. Hardesty, *Hilda: Ruler with Bishops, Lords, Kings* from "Great Women of Faith" (Eternity, 10/1974). See also Joan Morris, *The Lady Was a Bishop* (Macmillan, N.Y., 1973): "In the 4th century there were 20,000 nuns to only 10,000 monks. . . . The Basilian order was not founded by St. Basil but by his sister, Macrina."

[2] Lee Anna Starr, D.D., LL.D., *The Bible Status of Women*, op. cit., p. 377

[3] Victoria Booth Demarest, *What I Saw in Europe* (Vantage, Inc., N.Y., 1953)

[4]W. T. Stead, *Life of Mrs. Booth*, op. cit.

[5]Galatians 5:1

[6]Lee Anna Starr, op. cit., p. 377-79

[7]W. T. Stead, Op. Cit.

[8]Lee Anna Starr, Op. Cit., p. 386

[9]Anna Adams Gordon, *Frances E. Willard* (National Woman's Christian Temperance Union, Evanston, Ill., 1921).

[10]F. Willard, *Glimpses of Fifty Years* (G. M. Smith, Boston, 1889). See also Starr, op. cit., p. 380, 81, and Strahan, *The Maréchale*, p. 238.

[11]L. A. Starr, Op. Cit., p. 388

[12]IBID

[13]See *N. Y. Times*, 9/8/69

CHAPTER SIX

[1]Daniel 5:1-30. See especially *The Jerusalem Bible*, (Doubleday, N. Y., 1966)

[2]John 12:21

[3]W. T. Stead, *Life of Mrs. Booth*, Op. Cit.

[4]Hebrews 10:15, 16; Romans 8:16

[5]Luke 9:25

[6]J. E. Neel, *La Tour de Constance* (La Cause, Neuilly, France). Also Charles Sagnier, *The Tower of Constance and her Prisoners* (1882); M. D. Benoit, *Marie Durand* (1885); Ch. Bost, *The Martyrs of Aigues-Mortes* (1923)

[7]T. C. Upham, *The Life of Madame Guyon* (H. R. Allenson, Ltd., London, 1908). Also *Sweet Smelling Myrrh*, the Autobiography of Madame Guyon (edited by Abbie C. Morrow, 1898)

[8]I Corinthians 4:15; Galatians 4:19

[9]See Number 3 above

[10]Woman's Pulpit, Vol. III, No. 1, July, 1926

[11]See Number 3 above

[12]P. W. Wilson, *General Evangeline Booth of the Salvation Army* (Charles Scribner's Sons, N.Y., 1948) p. 176. See also E. Booth, *Woman* (Fleming H. Revell, 1930).

[13]Corrie ten Boom, *The Hiding Place* (Bantam/Revell, 1971); *Tramp for the Lord*, (Pillar/Revell, 1976)

[14]James 1:17

[15]Matthew 25: 14-30

[16]Matthew 5:16

[17]Isaiah 2:17

[18]*Daily Light on the Daily Path: A Devotional Text Book for Every Day in the Year in the Very Words of the Scripture*, (Samuel Bagster & Sons, Ltd., London)

[19]Hannah Whitall Smith, *The Christian's Secret of a Happy Life* (Fleming H. Revell Co., N. J.)

[20]Booth-Tucker, *The Life of Catherine Booth*, Vol. I, Op. Cit.

[21]C. Bramwell Booth, *Catherine Booth — The Story of Her Loves*, Op. Cit., p. 450.

CHAPTER SEVEN

[1]James Strahan, *The Maréchale*, Op. Cit.
[2]The Review of the Churches, Feb. 1894
[3]Strahan, Op. Cit., p. 239
[4]Booth-Tucker, Life of C. Booth, Op. Cit.
[5]Susan Welty, *Look Up and Hope*, (Thomas Nelson & Sons, N. Y., 1961)
[6]Matthew 12: 43-46

CHAPTER EIGHT

[0]John 3:19
[1]Amos 8:1
[2]James Montgomery Boice, *The Great Need for Preaching*
(Christianity Today, 11/20/74)
[3]Donald Coggan (Christianity Today, 12/5/75)
[4]I John 4:8
[5]Matthew 4:4; Luke 4:4
[6]Luke 3:16
[7]Mark 12:30
[8]John 13:35
[9]Matthew 5:44
[10]Romans 13:10
[11]I Corinthians 13:2
[12]John 21:15-17
[13]Luke 6:46
[14]Matthew 25:41-43, RSV
[15]Matthew 25:45, N.E.B.
[16]Philippians 4:8
[17]Jim Wallis (Christianity Today, 9/27/74)
[18]*Changing Church Roles for Women*, (Christianity Today, 9/27/74) p. 42
[19]Romans 8:9
[20]I Cor. 3:16; 6:19, 20; Peter 2:5
[21]I Cor. 10:17; Eph. 2:16; 4:4-6
[22]Rev. 21:2
[23]John 19:34
[24]Eph. 1:13
[25]Being thrilled with her poem, *Oh Church of Christ*, which I found on top of
the piano in a church, I wrote Effie Hussey for permission to set it to music
and publish it in 1951. She wrote back that she would be delighted for me
to do so.
[26]Luke 19:10; John 3:17
[27]Hebrews 4:14
[28]John 20:21
[29]Luke 3:3, 4
[30]Samuel 2:18, 26, 35; Samuel 3:1-18

[31]C. S. Lewis, *God in the Dock: Essays on Theology and Ethics,* Edited by Walter Hooper (W. B. Erdmans Publishing Co., 1972) p. 234-239. (Originally published as an article, "Notes on the Way," on "Priestesses in the Church," *Time and Tide,* August 14, 1948)

[32]Isaiah 55:8

[33]Matthew 12:50

[34]Matthew 23:9

[35]Matthew 12:50

[36]John 3:29 and Rev. 21:2; 22:17

[37]I Cor. 12:21

[38]Tampa *Tribune* 9/15/75

[40]Acts 2:17, 18

[42]Karen Stone: "Antoinette Brown — 1825-1921, The *Episcopalian,* Jan., 1975

[43]New York *Times,* 6/7/76

[44]Winrich Scheffbuch, *Christianity under the Hammer,* (Zondervan, 1974)

[45]Winthrop Hudson, *Christianity Today,* 1/2/76

[46]Matthew 17:20

[47]Eph. 6:13-17

[48]Acts 26:18

BIBLIOGRAPHY

BIBLE TRANSLATIONS

1. *The Holy Bible:* Authorized King James Version (Oxford University Press, London)
   All Biblical references in this volume are taken from this translation unless otherwise specified.

2. *The New Testament in Modern English,* Helen Barrett Montgomery, translator (American Baptist Publication Society, The Judson Press, Philadelphia, 1924)

3. *The Living Bible, Paraphrased* (Tyndale House Publishers, Wheaton, Illinois, 1971)

4. *The Holy Bible,* The Scofield Reference Bible (Oxford University Press, 1909)

5. *The Holy Bible,* Revised Standard Version (Thomas Nelson & Sons, New York, 1952)

6. *The Holy Bible from Eastern Manuscripts,* George M. Lamsa (A. J. Holman Company, Philadelphia, 1957)

7. *The Amplified Bible,* (Zondervan Publishing House, Grand Rapids, Michigan, 1965)

8. *The New Testament in Modern English,* J. B. Phillips (MacMillan Company, New York, 1959)

9. *The New Testament, An American Translation,* Edgar J. Goodspeed (The University of Chicago Press, 1909)

10. *Good News for Modern Man,* (American Bible Society, New York, 1966)

11. *The Jerusalem Bible,* (Doubleday and Company, New York, 1966)

12. *The Woman's Bible,* (according to Dr. Adiel Moncrief, editor of "Religion in Today's World," it may have been privately published around the year 1880, in only two editions. The Public Library of St. Petersburg has no information).

BIBLIOGRAPHY

RECOMMENDED BOOKS AND ARTICLES

1. *The Life of Catherine Booth, Mother of the Salvation Army (Vol. I, II)* by Frederick de Lautour Booth-Tucker, (Fleming H. Revell Co. 1892)

2. *Catherine Booth*, Catherine Bramwell Booth (Hodder and Stoughton, Ltd., London, 1970).

3. *The Church and Woman,* Rev. Maude Royden (James Clark and Co., Long, George H. Doran Co., N. Y., 1926).

4. *God's Word to Women*, Katherine Bushnell (Privately published, 1912)

5. *The Bible Status of Women*, Lee Anna Starr, D.D., LL.D. (Fleming H. Revell, N. Y., 1926)

6. *The Creation*, James Weldon Johnson; see A. Adolf, "The Poetry of Black America" (Harper and Row, 1973).

7. *Milton the Awakener*, Virginia Ramey Mollenkort (Christianity Today, 11/8/74).

8. *Great Women of Faith*, Nancy Hardesty (Eternity Today, 12/74)

9. *Joan of Arc*, Mark Twain, (Harper and Row, N. Y. 1896)

10. *Life of Mrs. Booth*, W. T. Stead, (Fleming H. Revell, 1900).

11. *Harmony of the Gospels*, John Broadus, (Hodder and Stoughton, N. Y. George H. Doran Co., 1903).

12. *The Greater Men and Women of the Bible*, Dr. James Hastings, (Scribner's, N. Y. 1916 Vol. I-VI).

13. *What I Saw in Europe*, Victoria Booth Demarest, D.D. (Vantage Press, N. Y., 1953).

14. *The Life of Frances E. Willard*, Anna Adams Gordon, (National Woman's Christian Temperance Union, Evanston, Ill., 1921).

15. *Glimpses of Fifty Years*, Frances Willard (publisher unknown).

16. *The Maréchale*, James Strahan, (Hodder and Stoughton, London, 1914).

17. *General Evangeline Booth of the Salvation Army*, R. W. Wilson, (Charles Scribner's Sons, N. Y., 1948).

18. *Catherine Booth — The Story of Her Loves*, Catherine Bramwell Booth, (Hodder and Stoughton, London, 1970).

19. *The New International Dictionary of the Christian Church*, J. D. Douglas, General Editor, (Zondervan Publishing House, 1974).

20. *All We're Meant to Be, A Biblical Approach to Women's Liberation*, Letha Scanzoni, Nancy Hardesty, (Word Books, Texas, 1974).

21. *Look Up and Hope*, Susan Welty, (Thoman Nelson and Sons, N. Y., 1961).

22. *The Life of Madame Guyon*, T. C. Upham, H. R. Allenson, LTD., London, 1908).

23. *Sweet Smelling Myrrh, the Autobiography of Madame Guyon*, edited by Abbie C. Morrow, 1898).

24. *Daily Light on the Daily Path:* A Devotional Textbook for everyday in the year in the Very Words of the Scripture, (Samuel Bagster and Sons, Ltd., London).

25. *The Lady Was a Bishop*, The hidden history of Women with clerical ordination and the Jurisdiction of Bishops, Joan Morris, (MacMillan Co., N. Y., 1973).

26. *The Church and the Second Sex*, Mary Daley (Harper and Row, New York, 1968)

27. *Women Priests, Yes or No?* Emily C. Hewitt and Suzanne R. Hiatt (Seabury Press, New York, 1973)

28. *The Hiding Place*, Corrie ten Boom with John and Elizabeth Sherrill (Fleming Revell and Bantam Books, 1971)

29. *Tramp for the Lord*, Corrie ten Boom with Jamie Buckingham (Fleming Revell and Pillar Books, 1976)

30. *Woman*, Evangeline Booth (Fleming Revell Company, New York, MCMIII)

31. *Dictionary of the Bible*, edited by James Hastings, D.D., (Charles Scribner's Sons, New York, 1940)

32. *The History of the Church of Christ*, Rev. Joseph Milner, A.M. (Hogan & Thompson, Philadelphia, 1835)

33. *The Life of General William Booth, The Founder of the Salvation Army*, Harold Begbie (MacMillan Company, New York, 1920)

34. *Soldiers Without Swords*, Herbert A. Wisbey, Jr. (MacMillan Company, New York, 1955)

35. *They Endured*, The Maréchale (Marshall, Morgan & Scott, Ltd., London, 1950)

36. *What of the Women*, Cynthia Wedel, (Episcopal Church).

37. *The Glorious Liberty*, Cynthia Wedel, (Church Women United).

38. *Employed Women and the Church*, Cynthia Wedel, (Church Women United).

39. *Happy Issue*, Janet Tilloch and Cynthia Wedel, (Seabury Press).

40. *Changing Patterns for Church Women*, Cynthia Wedel, (Forward Movement, Cincinatti, Ohio).

41. *Prayer Dialogue*, Cynthia Wedel, (Forward Movement, Ohio).

42. *Faith or Fear and Future Shock*, Cynthia Wedel, (Friendship Press, 1974).

43. *Foundations of Christian Knowledge*, Georgia Harkness, (Abington Press, Nashville, Tenn. 1955).

44. *The Christian's Secret of a Happy Life*, Hannah Whitall Smith, (Fleming H. Revell Co., New Jersey).

45. *Neither Male Nor Female, A Study of the Scriptures*, Q. M. Adams, Christ for the Nations, Dallas, Texas, 1973.

46. *Man As Male and Female*, Paul K. Jewett. William B. Erdmans Publishing Co., Grand Rapids, Mi., 1975.

47. *Women, Men and the Bible*, Virginia Ramey Mollenkott, Abingdon Press, Nashville, Tenn., 1977.

182